Assisted Reproduction, Discrimination, and the Law

The numbers of women undergoing Assisted Reproduction Technology (ART) treatments have risen steadily, yet they remain largely outside the scope of equality and employment law protection while undergoing treatment. *Assisted Reproduction, Discrimination, and the Law* examines this gap in UK law, with reference to EU law as appropriate, and argues that new conceptions of equality are necessary. Drawing from the literature on multidimensional and intersectional discrimination, it is argued that an intersectionality approach offers a more useful analytical framework to extend protection to those engaged in ART treatments. Drawing from Schiek's intersectional nodes model, the book critically examines two alternative interpretations of existing protected characteristics, namely infertility as a disability, with reference to the social model of disability and the UN Convention on the Rights of Persons with Disabilities 2006, and redefining the boundaries of pregnancy and/or sex discrimination, with reference to attempts to extend associative discrimination to pregnancy. Comparisons are drawn with the US, where infertility has been recognised as a disability under the Americans with Disabilities Act 1990 and as a pregnancy-related condition under the Pregnancy Discrimination Act 1978. A specific right to paid time off work to undergo treatment is also proposed, drawing comparisons with the US Family and Medical Leave Act 1993 and the existing UK work-family rights framework. It is argued that the reinterpretations of equality law and the rights proposed here are not only conceptually possible but could practically be achieved with minor, but significant, amendments to existing legislation.

Dr Michelle Weldon-Johns is a lecturer in Employment Law at Abertay University in Dundee. Her specific research interest is the boundaries between work and family life from UK and EU employment and equality law perspectives. Her research focuses on gender equality and the work-family conflict, particularly from the perspectives of working fathers and atypical working families. She has also written on the potential implications of Brexit for Scotland in the employment and work-family context.

Assisted Reproduction, Discrimination, and the Law

Michelle Weldon-Johns

Routledge
Taylor & Francis Group

LONDON AND NEW YORK

First published 2020
by Routledge
2 Park Square, Milton Park, Abingdon, Oxon OX14 4RN

and by Routledge
605 Third Avenue, New York, NY 10017

First issued in paperback 2021

Routledge is an imprint of the Taylor & Francis Group, an informa business

Publisher's Note
The publisher has gone to great lengths to ensure the quality of this reprint but points out that some imperfections in the original copies may be apparent.

British Library Cataloguing-in-Publication Data
A catalogue record for this book is available from the British Library

Library of Congress Cataloging-in-Publication Data
Names: Weldon-Johns, Michelle, author.
Title: Assisted reproduction, discrimination, and the law /
  Dr. Michelle Weldon-Johns.
Description: Abingdon, Oxon ; New York, NY Routledge, 2020. |
  Includes bibliographical references and index.
Identifiers: LCCN 2019041327 (print) | LCCN 2019041328
  (ebook) | ISBN 9781138610040 (hardback) | ISBN
  9780429465895 (ebook)
Subjects: LCSH: Pregnant women—Legal status, laws, etc.—
  Great Britain. | Human reproductive technology—Law
  and legislation—Great Britain. | Sex discrimination in
  employment—Law and legislation—Great Britain.
Classification: LCC KD3103.W6 W45 2020 (print) | LCC
  KD3103.W6 (ebook) | DDC 346.4101/7—dc23
LC record available at https://lccn.loc.gov/2019041327
LC ebook record available at https://lccn.loc.
  gov/2019041328

ISBN 13: 978-1-03-224020-6 (pbk)
ISBN 13: 978-1-138-61004-0 (hbk)

Typeset in Galliard
by Apex CoVantage, LLC

For Scott, Jessica and Logan.

Contents

1 Introduction

Introduction

Research published by the Human Fertilisation and Embryology Authority (HFEA) in May 2019 showed that the number of assisted reproduction technologies (ART) treatments undertaken in the UK has risen steadily since 1990.[1] These data show that in 2017, 54,760 patients underwent 75,425 treatments, indicating that some underwent multiple treatment cycles. These included 69,822 cycles of in vitro fertilisation (IVF), 5,603 cycles of intrauterine injection (IUI) in the form of donor insemination, 1,462 egg-freezing cycles, 581 egg-thaw cycles, 690 pre-implementation genetic diagnosis treatment cycles and 447 egg-sharing cycles,[2] and this does not capture pre-treatment assessment undertaken to investigate and diagnose infertility issues in the first instance. For those undergoing treatment aimed at facilitating conception, only 22% of IVF and 14% of IUI treatments were successful.[3] This, in part, explains why some patients underwent multiple treatment cycles. These figures represent an increasing number of women utilising ART treatments for various reasons, including extending and/or protecting reproductive capacity and, primarily, to become pregnant. While the vast majority were in heterosexual couples (90.7%), there is an increasing diversity of partner status of patients which includes female same-sex couples (5.9%), single women (3%) and surrogates (0.4%).[4] This indicates that recourse to ART treatments is an increasingly normalised route to parenthood and is likely to continue to increase in the future.

1 Human Fertilisation and Embryology Authority, 'HEFA Fertility Treatment: Trends and Figures 2017' (HFEA 2019) 17–19.
2 *Ibid*, 18–19.
3 *Ibid*, 22.
4 *Ibid*, 9, 13.

While this is not solely a question of infertility, this continues to be the primary reason for undergoing treatment. Infertility is often perceived as a woman's 'fault'[5] and her responsibility to remedy.[6] This is reflective of the fact that treatments are asymmetrical in nature with women undergoing the most invasive and prolonged procedures.[7] Consequently, women bear the significant physical, mental and emotional strains, burdens and risks of undergoing treatment from the investigatory stages throughout ART treatments and then during the much-desired pregnancy should treatment be successful. While it could be argued that undergoing ART treatments is a 'choice' for which those engaging in it have accepted to bear the risks, this fails to understand the responsibility that a woman may feel to undertake such treatment, particularly where the issue lies with her partner.[8] It also fails to appreciate the lack of alternative options for same-sex couples who wish to have a child that is biologically related to one of them. In addition, pressures within society for women and couples to have a child and the continued stigma of being involuntarily childless that many women face also contribute to decisions to undergo treatment.[9] While it can be argued that the pressure to become a mother is underpinned by patriarchal assumptions about women's role and social identity,[10] involuntary childlessness is nevertheless the fundamental reason why those engaged in ART treatments are doing so.[11] Fundamentally, those who choose to undergo ART treatments do so for the simple reason that they want to have a child that is biologically related to them.

Aside from these burdens and risks, working women face the dual burdens of undergoing treatment while balancing paid employment. Deech

---

5 Deborah K Dallmann, 'The Lay View of What "Disability" Means Must Give Way to What Congress Says It Means: Infertility as a "Disability" Under the Americans with Disabilities Act' [1996] 38(1) Wm & Mary L Rev 371, 386–87; Ruth Deech and Anna Smajdor, *From IVF to Immortality: Controversy in the Era of Reproductive Technology* (OUP 2007) 13; Arthur Greil, Julia McQuillan, and Kathleen Slauson Blevins, 'The Social Construction of Infertility' [2011] 5(8) Sociology Compass 736.
6 Elizabeth A Sternke and Kathleen Abrahamson, 'Perceptions of Women with Infertility on Stigma and Disability' [2015] 33(3) Sex Disability 3, 5.
7 Deech and Smajdor (n.5), 20–21.
8 Sternke and Abrahamson (n.6).
9 Deech and Smajdor (n.5), 87–91; Rachel Anne Fenton, D Jane, V Rees and Sue Heenan, ' "Shall I Be Mother?" Reproductive Autonomy, Feminism and the Human Fertilisation and Embryology Act 2008' in Jackie Jones, Anna Grear, Rachel Anne Fenton and Kim Stevenson (eds), *Gender, Sexualities and Law* (Routledge 2011) 242–44; Sternke and Abrahamson (n.6).
10 For an overview see: Fenton, Rees and Heenan (n.9), 242–44.
11 Shorge Sato, 'A Little Bit Disabled: Infertility and the Americans with Disabilities Act' [2001] 5 Legislation and Public Policy 189, 201; *Ibid*.

and Smajdor note that the implications for time off work are not limited to actually undergoing treatment, which is time-sensitive and inflexible itself, but can also be related to the physical and psychological effects of undergoing treatment which require additional absences.[12] Consequently, women undergoing ART treatments are not only exposing themselves to the risks involved in undergoing treatment but also those related to taking continued time off work,[13] sometimes with little advanced notice. This is coupled with the lack of legal framework specifically aimed at protecting those undergoing ART treatments. In addition, while they may not wish to disclose this to their employer, often the circumstances themselves make it difficult to keep it secret. As Advocate General (AG) Colomer observed in (Case C-506/06) *Mayr v Bäckerei und Konditorei Gerhard Flöckner OHG*,

> Ms Mayr probably wished to keep her desire to conceive to herself. It would be quite reasonable to suppose that she would have preferred to keep this private and intimate matter a secret for a few months. But this was not possible as the assisted reproduction process to which she was obliged to have recourse made it necessary for her to disclose her secret immediately.[14]

As decisions within both the UK and the EU have shown, women undergoing ART treatments have only been able to secure equality law protection in very limited circumstances, where transfer is imminent.[15] These decisions exposed the limitations within the current equality law framework and the difficulty of interpreting existing protected characteristics to include those undergoing ART treatments. This is particularly problematic as the stages

12 Deech and Smajdor (n.5), 89. Recent research in the UK supports this: Nicola Payne, Susan Seenan and Olga van den Akker, 'Experiences and Psychological Distress of Fertility Treatment and Employment' [2019] 40(2) Journal of Psychosomatic Obstetrics & Gynecology 156, 162–63.
13 Sandra M. Tomkowicz, 'The Disabling Effects of Infertility: Fertile Grounds for Accommodating Infertile Couples under the Americans with Disabilities Act' [1995] 46 Syracuse L Rev 1051, 1088; Dallmann (n.5), 392; Cintra D. Bentley, 'A Pregnant Pause: Are Women Who Undergo Fertility Treatment to Achieve Pregnancy within the Scope of Title VII's Pregnancy Discrimination Act' [1998] 73 Chi-Kent L Rev 391; Teresa M. Abney, 'Working Women Seeking Infertility Treatments: Does the ADA or Title VII Offer Any Protection?' [2009] 58(1) Drake L Rev 295, 296; Sternke and Abrahamson (n.6), 5; Kerry Van der Burch, 'Courts' Struggle with Infertility: The Impact of *Hall v. Nalco* on Infertility-Related Employment Discrimination' [2010] 81 University of Colorado L Rev 545, 550–52.
14 [2008] 2 CMLR 27, [AG4].
15 *Ibid; Sahota v The Home Office* [2010] 2 CMLR 29.

involved are lengthy, complex and largely asymmetrical with women bearing the greatest burdens. The lack of legal protection during such time only exposes them to greater uncertainty and risk during a period which is already fraught with both.

A significant difficulty in this context is the diversity of those using ART treatment with the result that they do not fall within an easily defined group or protected characteristic. The primary connecting factor is that the recipient of the treatment is biologically female, with women being perceived as the 'primary interest holders in reproduction.'[16] However, as the HFEA data show, the reasons for undergoing treatment are varied. While these can be referred to broadly as fertility treatments, the inability to conceive naturally can be related to a range of factors. For instance, the woman undergoing treatment may have a fertility issue herself which may relate to an underlying disability that prevents and/or reduces the likelihood of her conceiving naturally and/or from maintaining a pregnancy. However, the fertility issue may relate to her partner and treatments are required to facilitate conception. Alternatively, it could relate to social factors, such as same-sex relationships or age-related fertility issues, that may be related to delaying parenthood,[17] or it could be entirely unexplained.[18] Consequently, the experiences of those undergoing ART treatments are varied and complex, not least of all because they have the potential to intersect with a variety of protected characteristics. This can raise practical and conceptual difficulties when attempting to include those undergoing ART treatments within the current equality law framework.

The diversity of those undergoing ART treatments reinforces the need to adopt alternative interpretations of the current boundaries within UK equality law. Consequently, the book draws from the literature on multidimensional and intersectional discrimination, particularly Schiek's intersectional nodes model.[19] It is argued that only by recognising complex and diverse social identities can equality law effectively reflect and respond to the increasingly diverse and intertwined disadvantages that individuals suffer because of their intersecting characteristics. This is keenly felt by those who undergo ART treatments because they represent a diverse group

16 Fenton, Rees and Heenan (n.9), 241.
17 *Ibid*, 243–44.
18 Marjorie Maguire Shultz, 'Reproductive Technology and Intent-Based Parenthood: An Opportunity for Gender Neutrality' [1990] Wis L Rev 297, 311–16.
19 Dagmar Schiek, 'Organizing EU Equality Law Around the Nodes of " 'Race", Gender and Disability' in Dagmar Schiek and Anna Lawson (eds), *European Union Non-Discrimination Law and Intersectionality: Investigating the Triangle of Racial, Gender and Disability Discrimination* (Ashgate Publishing 2011).

of women undergoing treatment for various reasons, some of which are not attributable to the woman herself. This is also closely tied with societal expectations of appropriate motherhood, biological roles and stigma around childlessness,[20] all of which are reinforced in the current equality and employment law frameworks which privilege traditional motherhood and pregnancy, only offering protections where alternatives most closely assimilate with this.[21] In doing so, it further problematises and marginalises those undergoing ART treatments.

One of three main lines of argument has been adopted by those experiencing less favourable treatment because of their engagement with ART treatments. All have argued that it relates to their sex, with a focus on the specifically gendered nature of treatment.[22] In addition, they either argue that it falls within the ambit of disability or pregnancy discrimination.[23] This mirrors the approaches adopted in the US, where the Americans with Disabilities Act 1990 (ADA) now includes reproduction as a major life activity and so impairments that limit this, including infertility, fall within its scope.[24] In addition, reference to pregnancy-related medical condition in the US Pregnancy Discrimination Act 1978 has been interpreted by some US courts to include undergoing ART treatments.[25] As outlined in Chapter 2 and discussed further in Chapters 3 and 4, both of these routes have been attempted in the UK and EU not only with no success but also with no meaningful consideration of the kinds of reasoning adopted in the US. While this book focuses on the UK, reference is made to the EU approach as appropriate, and comparisons are drawn with the experience in the US.

The US is an appropriate comparator for several reasons. Firstly, both have previously been classified as having low labour market regulation coupled with limited regulation of the family,[26] drawing similar boundaries

---

20 Sternke and Abrahamson (n.6).
21 This is most evident in cases on access to childcare rights: Case C-167/12 *CD v ST* [2014] 3 CMLR 15 and Case C-363/12 *Z v A (Re Equal Treatment)* [2014] 3 CMLR 20.
22 *Mayr* (n.14); *Sahota* (n.15).
23 *CD* (n.21); *Z* (n.21).
24 As amended by the ADA Amendments Act of 2008 Pub L No.110–325 122 Stat 3553.
25 Pub L No.95–555, 92 Stat 2076 (codified at 42 USC §2000e(k)). *Pacourek v Inland Steel Company* 858 F Supp 1393 (N.D. Ill. 1994); *Pacourek v Inland Steel Company* 916 F. Supp. 797 (N.D. Ill. 1996); *Erickson v Board of Governors of State Colleges*, 911 F Supp 316 (ND Ill 1995), 318–20; *Hall v Nalco Co.* 534 F 3d 644 (7th Cir 2008).
26 Gosta Esping-Andersen, *Social Foundations of Postindustrial Economies* (OUP 1999) 85–86; Diane Sainsbury, 'Women's and Men's Social Rights: Gendering Dimensions

between public and private spheres. This indicates that they would adopt similar approaches regarding employment and equality law. This is reflected in those areas of UK employment law that are not derived from EU law where the UK has adopted a de-regulatory approach[27] akin to that in the US. Secondly, the underpinning legislative frameworks contain similar protected characteristics that are framed in broadly comparable terms. This means that interpretations adopted in the US can meaningfully be compared with those in the UK. Indeed, in the drafting of the UK Disability Discrimination Act 1995 comparisons were drawn with the ADA.[28] Thirdly, the development of legislation and the interpretation of protected characteristics in the US all centre on the intersections of disability and gender/sex. This is similarly the case in the UK and EU contexts. While an intersectionality approach is not explicitly adopted in the US, it nevertheless reflects Schiek's intersecting nodes approach, particularly the intersections between gender and disability.[29] The comparison with the US thus facilitates the analysis and application of this intersectionality approach in the UK context.

While the easiest solution may appear to be to create a new protected characteristic relating to undergoing ART treatments, there are several important reasons why reinterpretation is preferred in the first instance. Firstly, the development and introduction of new protected characteristics have been piecemeal and challenging,[30] indicating that it is no easy task to add another to the list. Secondly, in many instances, where new protected characteristics have been enacted, they have developed from broader interpretations being given to existing ones in the first instance, for example pregnancy and gender reassignment.[31] This indicates that new characteristics are more likely to be recognised if they can be grounded in existing

---

of Welfare States' in Diane Sainsbury (ed), *Gendering Welfare State Regimes* (Sage Publications 1994) 165–66; Diane Sainsbury, *Gender, Equality and Welfare States* (CUP 1996) 68–69, 95–98.

27 Adrian Beecroft, *Report on Employment Law* (URN 12/825 2011).

28 Brian Doyle, 'Employment Rights, Equal Opportunities and Disabled Persons: The Ingredients for Reform' [1993] 22(2) IJL 89. It has also influenced EU developments: Gerard Quinn and Eilionóir Flynn, 'Transatlantic Borrowings: The Past and Future of EU Non-discrimination Law and Policy on the Ground of Disability' [2012] 60(1) The American Journal of Comparative Law 23.

29 Schiek (n.19).

30 Linda Dickens, 'The Road Is Long: Thirty Years of Equality Legislation in Britain' [2007] 45(3) British Journal of Industrial Relations 463, especially 464–74.

31 (C-177/88) *Dekker v Stichting Vormingscentrum voor Jonge Volwassenen Plus* [1992] ICR 325; (C-32/93) *Webb v EMO Air Cargo (UK) Ltd* [1994] 2 CMLR 729; (C13/94) *P v S and Cornwall County Council* [1996] 2 CMLR 247.

protections. Thirdly, recourse to an ever-expanding list has been criticised by those advocating for a multidimensional and/or intersectional approach to the future development of equality law.[32] This indicates that a more nuanced analysis of the interrelationship and intersections between characteristics is preferable to an enlarged list. Consequently, instead of proposing another protected characteristic, it is argued that the existing legislative framework provides the potential to be reinterpreted more broadly to include those undergoing ART treatments. Nevertheless, an alternative approach is presented in Chapter 5 which considers the possibility of a specific employment law right to time off work to undergo treatment.

The UK is also well-placed to make these changes as it has a highly regulated legal framework surrounding ART treatments. In addition, the legal framework surrounding surrogacy arrangements is currently being re-examined.[33] Ensuring the legal protection of those using surrogacy arrangements and undergoing ART treatments seems like a logical next step. Furthermore, while the Court of Justice of the European Union (CJEU) found it difficult to broaden the scope of protected characteristics, in part, because of the lack of consensus throughout Europe,[34] the same is not true in the UK context. The UK has recognised employment-related rights for commissioning parents in surrogacy.[35] The equality law framework is also already in place to facilitate multidimensional discrimination. Section 14 of the Equality Act 2010 (EqA), which has not been brought into force, allows for dual grounds in discrimination claims, which could be used to facilitate a multidimensional or intersectional approach should it ever be brought into force. In addition, the UK has committed itself to the UN Convention on Rights of Persons with Disabilities,[36] which should be considered when interpreting domestic law. These factors all indicate that the time is ripe to make these changes and develop a more coherent legal framework for those undergoing ART treatments. Before turning to focus on the gaps within the current equality law frameworks in Chapter 2, the

---

32 For a critique of the grounds-based approach see: Aileen McColgan, 'Reconfiguring Discrimination Law' [2007] (SPR) PL 74.

33 Law Commission, *Thirteenth Programme of Law Reform* (Law Com No.377, 2017), 2.40–2.44; Scottish Law Commission, *Tenth Programme of Law Reform* (Law Com No.250, 2018) 2.32–2.37.

34 The diversity of both opinions and legal regulation of surrogacy arrangements and the significant divergence in approach between member states was noted by AG Wahl in *Z* (n.21), [AG1] and [AG37].

35 Children and Families Act 2014; Michelle Weldon-Johns, 'From Modern Workplaces to Modern Families – Re-envisioning the Work – Family Conflict' [2015] 37(4) JSWFL 395.

36 Convention on the Rights of Persons with Disabilities 2007 [A/RES/61/106].

legal framework surrounding ART treatments and the treatments included within the definition used here are outlined.

ART treatments

In the UK, those providing ART treatments are overseen by HFEA,[37] which is regulated by the Human Fertilisation and Embryology Act 1990 (HFEA 1990).[38] The legislation also outlines the legal consequences of treatment in terms of family status for those involved,[39] and the parameters of permitted embryology research.[40] The legislation has been subject to much academic scrutiny over the years,[41] particularly relating to the legal consequences for parenthood and the limiting impact it previously had on certain family forms,[42] all of which is beyond the scope of this book. However, it is clear that those providing ART treatments are highly regulated by the legislation,[43] as are the legal consequences of successful treatment in terms of parental status.[44]

The current legal framework does not drawn distinctions between the reasons for wanting to utilise ART treatments, although medical judgements are used on the suitability of treatment in individual cases.[45] Nevertheless, those undergoing treatment are also covered by the EqA as service users.[46] As such, they must not be discriminated against by being treated less favourably on the grounds of any of the protected characteristics in the

37 It has regulatory, licensing, advisory and policy-making functions. HFEA 1990, s.8.
38 *Ibid*, ss.5–22.
39 *Ibid*, ss.27–29.
40 *Ibid*, ss.3–4A (relevant parts), 11, 14–15, 41, Sch.2 paras.1, 3–4, Sch.3 paras.2, 4, 6–7.
41 Marie Fox, 'The Human Fertilisation and Embryology Act 2008: Tinkering at the Margins' [2009] 17 (3) Fem LS 333; Rachel Anne Fenton, Susan Heenan and Jane Rees, 'Finally Fit for Purpose? The Human Fertilization and Embryology Act 2008' [2010] 32(3) JSWFL 275; Kirsty Horsey (ed), *Revisiting the Regulation of Human Fertilisation and Embryology* (Routledge 2015).
42 Fenton, Heenan and Rees (n.41), 278–80; Julie McCandless and Sally Sheldon, 'The Human Fertilisation and Embryology Act (2008) and the Tenacity of the Sexual Family Form' [2010] 73(2) MLR 175.
43 Kirsty Horsey, 'Revisiting the Regulation of Human Fertilisation and Embryology' in Kirsty Horsey (ed), *Revisiting the Regulation of Human Fertilisation and Embryology* (Routledge 2015) 2–3.
44 For a discussion of the Human Fertilisation and Embryology Act 2008 amendments see: Fox (n.41); Fenton, Heenan and Rees (n.41); McCandless and Sheldon (n.42); Fenton, Rees and Heenan (n.9).
45 Fox (n.41), 337; Fenton, Heenan and Rees (n.41), 278.
46 EqA, ss.28–29.

provision, or refusal, of treatment.[47] Consequently, the diversity of those seeking such treatment is largely accepted in terms of access and the legal consequences of treatment.[48] Despite this, and the resultant normalisation of ART treatments,[49] gaps remain for those undergoing treatment from an employment and equality law perspective. This is even more problematic when the nature of treatments, and their impact on employment, is considered.

ART covers a range of treatments and procedures, however, before any of these are embarked on, there are a variety of investigatory procedures required to determine the nature of the infertility and the most effective treatment. This itself can take time and is generally far more onerous and invasive for women than for men. For men, the main tests involve semen analysis and chlamydia testing, both of which are non-invasive and require limited time off work. In the first instance, women also undergo non-invasive testing for chlamydia and a series of blood tests to determine if ovulation is occurring. While both are non-invasive, blood tests must be taken on specific days and may be repeated, thus potentially requiring time off work. Further testing for women becomes increasingly more invasive and likely to impact on work. This can include transvaginal ultrasounds to check the womb, uterus and fallopian tubes; hysterosalpingogram, which involves an x-ray of the womb and fallopian tubes following the injection of a dye to investigate whether there are any blockages; and a laparoscopy, which is keyhole surgery involving a small incision being made in the lower tummy and insertion of a thin tube with a camera enabling the womb, fallopian tubes and ovaries to be investigated for blockages.[50] All of these are invasive, can cause discomfort and are likely to involve taking some time off work.

The treatments themselves vary in complexity and the stages involved prior to the final transfer or insemination occurring but are again asymmetrical in nature. Broadly speaking, they cover the use of fertility drugs, IUI, IVF and surrogacy arrangements.[51] Fertility drugs may be used alone

---

47 *Ibid*, ss.4–12: age, discrimination, gender reassignment, marriage and civil partnership, race, religion or belief, sex and sexual orientation.
48 With the exception of age: NICE guidelines limiting access to those under 40, with only one cycle of treatment recommended for women between 40–42 if they have never had treatment before: NICE, Fertility problems: assessment and treatment, Clinical guideline [CG156], <www.nice.org.uk/guidance/cg156/chapter/ Recommendations#access-criteria-for-ivf> accessed 30 July 2019, 1.11.
49 Fox (n.41), 335.
50 More details on these procedures can be found on the NHS website: <www.nhs.uk/ conditions/infertility/diagnosis/> accessed 30 July 2019.
51 See the HFEA website for more details on treatments currently covered in the UK: <www.hfea.gov.uk/treatments/explore-all-treatments/> accessed 30 July 2019.

or in conjunction with other treatments. They can be used to correct hormone imbalances in both men and women and to increase the likelihood of pregnancy occurring. While relatively non-invasive, they can have a range of physical side-effects.[52] IUI is relatively straightforward and involves the highest-quality sperm, from either a donor or a partner/husband, being injected directly into the uterus when the woman ovulates. This requires monitoring the woman's cycle to determine when ovulation occurs and may involve using fertility drugs to optimise ovulation and the chance of success. While it is a comparatively simple procedure, it has a very low success rate, and multiple cycles are likely to be required, with related time off work also being necessary.[53]

IVF is much more complex, and the treatment is significantly more onerous and time-consuming, particularly for women. In this instance, both the eggs and the sperm are retrieved and are fertilised outside the body. Retrieval of sperm may be surgical but only where the sperm count is very low or where it has abnormal mobility.[54] While this is likely to involve time off work, it is still shorter in comparison with the treatment women undergo. Fertility drugs are used to regulate the woman's cycle, first to prevent ovulation and then to stimulate the ovaries to produce multiple eggs. The development of eggs is closely monitored using blood tests and ultrasounds, and once they are ready to be harvested, another drug is administered to ripen them. They are then removed between 30 to 40 hours later. The eggs are then mixed with the sperm in the hope that fertilisation will occur. In the meantime, the woman is undertaking a new course of fertility drugs to prepare the uterus for pregnancy. If fertilisation occurs, the most viable embryos are selected and transferred to the woman's uterus. This will normally be between two and six days following fertilisation. The fertility drug treatments continue until it is possible to determine if the transfer has been successful.[55] While this is more successful that IUI, the success rate is still only around 29% for those younger than 35.[56] This again suggests that multiple cycles will be attempted, with multiple periods of absence required.

---

52 HFEA, Fertility Drugs: <www.hfea.gov.uk/treatments/explore-all-treatments/fertility-drugs/> accessed 30 July 2019.

53 HFEA, Intrauterine Insemination (IUI): <www.hfea.gov.uk/treatments/explore-all-treatments/intrauterine-insemination-iui/> accessed 30 July 2019.

54 In this instance, intra-cytoplasmic sperm injection is used, where one sperm is injected directly into the egg. The other stages are the same.

55 Deech and Smajdor (n.5), 17–20.

56 Human Fertilisation and Embryology Authority, 'Fertility Treatment 2014–2016 Trends and Figures' (HFEA, March 2018) 15.

For surrogacy arrangements, IUI or IVF will be used with the surrogate either using her own eggs and the sperm of the intended father (partial surrogacy) or using the embryos of the intended parents (full surrogacy).[57] The likelihood of success is based on the kind of treatment and the quality of the genetic materials used. The relatively low success rates mean that those undergoing ART treatments are likely to undertake multiple treatment cycles before achieving a successful pregnancy or before deciding to end treatment. This is all likely to have the biggest impact on women receiving treatment, including their ability to reconcile this with paid employment.

Assisted reproduction, discrimination and the law

The experience of those undergoing ART treatments shows that an increasing number of women are undertaking procedures either with the hope of achieving pregnancy or in an attempt to preserve their fertility. For women, this can have a significant impact on their working lives. While the UK legislative framework has developed to recognise the changing routes to parenthood, the employment and equality law frameworks have lagged behind. This is not the only time when family law and employment law have failed to respond effectively to one another, being equally true in the context of work-family rights.[58] Nevertheless, inroads have been made in the context of commissioning parents in surrogacy, and the time is ripe to do so in this context too.

This book argues specifically for a broadening of the equality law framework to include those undergoing ART treatments, including commissioning parents in surrogacy. A specific right to time off work to undergo treatments is also presented as either an alternative or supplementary right to ensure employment protection in the pre-conception period, which is currently largely outside of the scope of legal protection. This includes those undergoing investigatory treatments relating to potential fertility issues and extends to all forms of treatment that individuals are personally engaged in. In this respect, the definition of those undergoing ART treatments includes commissioning parents in surrogacy situations insofar as they are undergoing treatment themselves. For instance, where the surrogate is to be implanted with embryos created by the commissioning

---

57 HFEA, Surrogacy: <www.hfea.gov.uk/treatments/explore-all-treatments/surrogacy/> accessed 30 July 2019.
58 Weldon-Johns (n.36); Nicole Busby and Michelle Weldon-Johns, 'Fathers as Carers in UK Law and Policy: Dominant Ideologies and Lived Experience' [2019] 41(3) JSWFL 280, 293.

parents, they would fall within this definition while undergoing treatment. They are also included insofar as they experience less favourable treatment and/or dismissal for a reason related to having recourse to ART treatments.

Chapter overviews

The book is arranged in four main chapters. Chapter 2 critically outlines the limitations of the UK legal frameworks in the UK, and in the EU, for those involved in ART treatments. Three protected characteristics (sex, disability and pregnancy, including where they intersect) are identified as those most capable of being reinterpreted and/or redefined to include those undergoing ART treatments. The literature on multidimensional and intersectional discrimination is reviewed to provide the analytical framework necessary to broaden the scope of equality law, with Schiek's intersectional nodes model being identified as providing a useful analytical framework in this context. Chapter 3 uses this framework to critically examine whether the UK definition of disability can be reinterpreted to include infertility as a disability. Different models of disability and how they relate to infertility are first examined before analysing the US jurisprudence through the lens of Schiek's intersectional nodes of disability and gender. This analysis shows that the closer the correlation between these grounds of discrimination, the more likely it is that protection is afforded. This analysis is then used to examine whether extending the boundaries of disability in the UK is possible. Chapter 4 critically considers redefining the boundaries of pregnancy and/or sex discrimination to include the broader concept of childbearing capacity. Schiek's model is again used to examine the US jurisprudence, this time focusing on gender intersecting with disability in the sense of requiring accommodation. This again shows similar correlations between recognising sex-specific childbearing capacity and including those undergoing treatment within the scope of pregnancy-related discrimination. This analysis is used to re-examine the boundaries of pregnancy and sex discrimination in the UK. This chapter also critically examines two low-level Scottish cases which have attempted to extend associative discrimination on the grounds of sex to include discrimination relating to someone else's pregnancy. In doing so, it considers whether this offers any possibilities to extend the scope of protection to include commissioning parents in surrogacy and/or those undergoing ART treatments. Chapter 5 looks beyond the equality law framework and proposes a right to time off work to undergo treatment as an alternative or supplementary approach to redefining the boundaries of equality law. Comparisons are again drawn with the US Family and

Medical Leave Act 1993,[59] as well as with current UK work-family rights, and it is argued that such a right would be conceptually and practically consistent with existing work-family rights. Finally, conclusions are drawn with recommendations for the future development of rights for those engaged in ART treatments.

59 Public Law 103–3107 Stat 6.

2 Current conceptions of equality and the limitations for those involved in assisted reproduction

Introduction

In this chapter, the decisions of the UK courts and the CJEU concerning those involved in ART treatments are critically examined to identify the main challenges and barriers within existing equality law frameworks. The gaps within the current legal framework are examined in two main contexts: the pre-conception period and access to childcare rights. While this analysis identifies the current limitations, it also indicates the possibilities for redefining the boundaries of the current protected characteristics in the future. The literature on multidimensional and intersectional discrimination is then examined as an alternative to the current individualised protected characteristic approach. Adopting an intersectional approach is useful because it recognises increasingly diverse social identities, which is particularly evident in the diversity of those undergoing ART treatments. It also enables new challenges to be recognised, allowing for a meaningful development of equality law to respond to these challenges. In particular, it is argued that Schiek's intersectional nodes approach offers a useful intersectional analytical lens through which to reinterpret the boundaries of the protected characteristics engaged here.

Pre-conception protection: the limitations of EU and UK law

The boundaries of equality law protection for those undergoing ART treatments were first tested in the UK in *London Borough of Greenwich v Robinson*.[1] In this case, Robinson had undergone three cycles of fertility treatment

---

1 (unreported; [1995] UKEAT 745), <www.bailii.org/uk/cases/UKEAT/1995/745_94_2111.html> accessed 30 July 2019.

when a redundancy situation arose, with sickness absence identified as the operative criterion for selection. It was determined that Robinson's was the highest, with most absences relating to undergoing IVF treatment.[2] Robinson consequently accepted voluntary redundancy, although she had unsuccessfully raised a grievance regarding the inclusion of IVF-related absences in the calculation. Her complaints to the Industrial Tribunal (IT) of unfair dismissal and unlawful discrimination on the grounds of sex were upheld. The majority noted that women were in a unique position while undergoing ART treatments and that any less favourable treatment on this basis amounted to sex discrimination.[3] Such an approach suggests that the IT accepted that as ART treatments are asymmetrical, with women bearing the greatest burden relating to their childbearing capacity, including related absences from work, any less favourable treatment in relation to undergoing IVF was necessarily on the grounds of sex. Unfortunately, the IT did not expand on its reasoning here. In addition, while this appeared to relate to direct discrimination, it then turned to discuss indirect discrimination in more depth.[4] A direct discrimination approach would have been more effective and would have reflected that adopted in relation to the development of pregnancy discrimination.[5] However, this was not accepted by the Employment Appeal Tribunal (EAT) and was overturned on appeal.[6]

Despite it being argued that undergoing IVF treatment was not analogous with illness, since pregnancy itself cannot be considered as a pathological condition,[7] the EAT held that it was. Justice Keene reasoned that infertility was a medical condition which, at times, required sickness leave to undergo medical treatments. Consequently, it should be treated in the same way as any other form of illness absence. Comparisons were made with other forms of sex-specific illnesses and the undesirability of treating them differently. Consequently, the EAT allowed the appeal, underscoring that less favourable treatment relating to undergoing ART treatments did not amount to unlawful sex discrimination. It is worth noting that it was not argued before the IT that undergoing IVF treatment was a pregnancy-related illness, which was one of the exceptions to the absence calculation, although Robinson had initially raised this point with her employer.

2 Absences relating to the miscarriage were not included in the final calculation.
3 *Robinson* (n.1).
4 *Ibid.*
5 (C-177/88) Dekker v Stichting Vormingscentrum voor Jonge Volwassenen Plus [1992] ICR 325; (C-32/93) Webb v EMO Air Cargo (UK) Ltd [1994] 2 CMLR 729.
6 However, the claim of unfair dismissal was upheld.
7 *Robinson* (n.1). With reference to the decision in *Webb* (n.5).

Therefore, the extent to which undergoing ART treatments could be compared with pregnancy and/or childbearing capacity remained to be determined. This issue was raised in the much later CJEU decision in Case C-506/06 *Mayr v Bäckerei und Konditorei Gerhard Flöckner OHG*.[8]

Mayr was given notice of her dismissal while she was undergoing IVF treatment. Two days before she received the notice, she had a follicular puncture, and transfer of the fertilised ova was planned for three days later. Consequently, at the time of receiving the notice, an *in vitro* fertilised ova existed. Mayr argued that at the date of notification, she was covered by pregnancy dismissal protection.[9] While the Austrian Court of first instance accepted that pregnancy began at the point of fertilisation and held that she was covered by dismissal protection, this was overturned by the appellate Court.[10] It reasoned that pregnancy could not exist independently of the female body and thus could only begin following transfer. Given the uncertainty regarding when pregnancy protection begins, the case was referred to the CJEU for a preliminary ruling on the meaning of pregnant worker within the Pregnant Workers Directive (PWD).[11]

Both the AG Opinion and the CJEU were mindful of the potentially far-reaching implications of deciding when pregnancy begins from a medical-ethical point of view. Thus, they were keen to stress that the case was limited to determining, from a legal point of view, when pregnancy protection begins within the scope of the PWD.[12] Having considered the traditional medical views, AG Colomer accepted that there were two possible points when pregnancy could begin: conception and implantation.[13] He reasoned that implantation is the point at which legal protection begins; as such, an approach is also supported in various literature and traditional views on pregnancy.[14] While the CJEU did not specifically refer to this reasoning, its judgement follows the same approach. Consequently, both found that a woman undergoing treatment is not a pregnant worker under the PWD and not entitled to dismissal protection under Art.10.[15] Such an interpretation was further supported by the increased legal certainty

---

8   [2008] 2 CMLR 27.
9   *Ibid*, [16]–[21].
10 *Ibid*, [24]–[27].
11 *Ibid*, [28]. Council Directive 92/85/EEC of 19 October 1992 on the introduction of measures to encourage improvements in the safety and health at work of pregnant workers and workers who have recently given birth or are breastfeeding.
12 *Ibid*, [AG6], [AG29], [38].
13 *Ibid*, [AG30]–[AG33].
14 *Ibid*, [AG33]–[AG38].
15 *Ibid*, [AG48], [41], [53].

it provided, particularly since transfer can be postponed and/or fertilised ova can be stored for up to 10 years in some member states,[16] with the related implication that pregnancy protection would extend throughout that period. AG Colomer also noted that focusing on fertilisation could mean that a woman was afforded pregnancy protection even when she used a surrogate.[17] It is perhaps not unexpected that the AG and the CJEU adopted this view on the scope of pregnancy protection, particularly given the diversity in approaches towards ART treatments throughout Europe and the conceptual difficulty of separating the beginning of pregnancy from the female body. However, some of the other points are more difficult to reconcile. For instance, it is notable that the Court mentions that the reason for dismissal protection is to avoid the 'harmful effects on the physical and mental state of pregnant workers.'[18] Given the similarly vulnerable position of those undergoing treatment, it is not clear how such a distinction can be drawn on this basis.

Nevertheless, AG Colomer noted that protection could be found in other areas of EU law.[19] Thus, Mayr was provided another opportunity to consider whether protection could be afforded, namely under the former Equal Treatment Directive, Directive 76/207.[20] While the applicability of Directive 76/207 was not raised by the referring Court, both the AG and the CJEU determined that it was also appropriate to consider it,[21] thus making a positive move to ensure protection here. Having reviewed the jurisprudence on pregnancy and pregnancy-related illness, AG Colomer suggested that it would be consistent with the legislation and this jurisprudence to extend protection under Directive 76/207 to the circumstances at hand.[22] The CJEU accepted this, and both held that dismissal of a female worker because she was undergoing sex-specific IVF treatment amounted to direct discrimination on the grounds of sex.[23] This is consistent with the approach adopted by the IT in *Robinson*. Indeed, the CJEU noted that failure to extend protection here would be contrary to the objectives

---

16 *Ibid*, [AG43]–[AG45], [42].
17 *Ibid*, [AG46].
18 *Ibid*, [39].
19 *Ibid*, [AG42].
20 Council Directive 76/207/EEC of 9 February 1976 on the implementation of the principle of equal treatment for men and women as regards access to employment, vocational training and promotion and working conditions.
21 *Mayr* (n.8), [AG50]–[AG51] and [43]–[44].
22 *Ibid*, [AG53]–[AG68].
23 *Ibid*, [AG68], [50].

underpinning Art.2(3) Directive 76/207.[24] In doing so, the Court took a bold step forward in recognising the potentially gendered elements of undergoing treatment with reference to general principles of equality, not just the sex discrimination provisions themselves.

However, the decision and the reasoning of the Court was criticised as being difficult to reconcile with that adopted in the earlier cases on pregnancy-related illness. For instance, Bell argues that this appears to draw distinctions between sex-specific medical treatment, which is afforded protection, and sex-specific illness, which is not. He argues that this boundary is 'fragile and tenuous . . . not least because sex-specific illnesses can give rise to sex-specific medical treatment.'[25] Had the Court articulated its reasoning more closely to childbearing capacity, this could have made the decision easier to reconcile. As Kilpatrick suggests, the decision can perhaps be explained by the close connection with pregnancy,[26] which had already been defined as direct sex discrimination. However, Kilpatrick notes that the justifications for pregnancy-related discrimination as direct sex discrimination are that pregnancy is female-specific, overcoming female disadvantage and public good. While the justifications for direct sex discrimination here are similar, she notes that they are not all the same.[27] There is no further elaboration on which ones are different, but given that treatment is predominately female-specific, and that protection would help overcome female disadvantage, particularly regarding reconciling treatment with work, the only other consideration is public good–related reasons. This may have reflected the diversity of opinions on ART treatments and the question of choice to undergo treatment. Given the diversity of those undergoing treatment and its increasing normalisation, there are clear reasons why closer comparisons with pregnancy and/or childbearing capacity, thus including it within the scope of direct sex discrimination, may be appropriate here.

Overall, the decision appeared to be a victory for those undergoing ART treatments, with scholars arguing that it was a bold step forward that would address the gaps in legal protection for those undergoing

---

24 *Ibid*, [51]. Now Art.28(1) Directive 2006/54/EC of the European Parliament and of the Council of 5 July 2006 on the implementation of the principle of equal opportunities and equal treatment of men and women in matters of employment and occupation (recast) (ETD).

25 Mark Bell, 'The Principle of Equal Treatment: Widening and Deepening' in Paul Craig and Gráinne De Búrca (eds), *The Evolution of EU Law* (OUP 2011), 617.

26 Claire Kilpatrick, 'The ECJ and Labour Law: A 2008 Retrospective' [2009] 38(2) ILJ 180, 190.

27 *Ibid*.

treatment.[28] However, there were also concerns about the wider implications of the decision and the potential for greater protection being afforded to those undergoing ART treatments, before pregnancy is even confirmed, than those conceiving naturally, thus creating a two-tier system.[29] While this is true, such an argument overlooks the reality that those undergoing ART treatments are in a noticeably different position to those conceiving naturally. The process of becoming pregnant using ART treatments is far more likely to impact on the ability to attend work, thus exposing them to less favourable treatment and/or discrimination in the pre-conception period. Greater protection is therefore necessary to ensure that those undergoing treatment can do so without fear of it impacting negatively on their workplace security. In any event, the CJEU framed the protection more narrowly, focusing on the facts at hand, to the very late stages of treatment, that is the period following follicular puncture when transfer is imminent.[30] While the Court must answer the specific question(s) referred to it, AG Colomer's Opinion also supports future narrow interpretations of the scope of this judgement:

> It is not a question of giving indefinite and armour-plated protection against dismissal to all . . . women who have a desire to have children, or even those who have started a long and painful course of assisted reproduction treatment, but of preventing employers acting in a manner contrary to either the principle of equality between men and women or the fundamental aim of protecting procreation which is of transcendental importance in any modern society.[31]

There are three points of note in this Opinion. Firstly, it recognises the fundamental societal value of procreation, thus suggesting some hope that the boundaries of protection will not be drawn too narrowly. Secondly, protection under Directive 76/207 is grounded in ensuring equal treatment between men and women in employment, thus, to some extent, recognising the different experiences in relation to childbearing and its impact on work. However, thirdly, it recognises that protection here is limited suggesting that it may not extend to all those undergoing ART treatments. This was confirmed in the subsequent UK case *Sahota v The Home Office*.[32]

---

28 Carol Fox, 'Protection in Contemplation of Pregnancy?' [2008] Emp LB 3, 3; Kilpatrick (n.26), 190.
29 Fox (n.28), 5.
30 *Mayr* (n.8), [52].
31 *Ibid*, [AG70].
32 [2010] 2 CMLR 29.

Sahota's absences, primarily relating to IVF treatment, triggered her employer's absence management policy. The policy expressly excluded periods of IVF treatment from the calculation; however, Sahota had provided insufficient documentation to support her claims that they were related to undergoing such treatment.[33] Consequently, her line manager first invited her to an informal meeting to discuss this and provide the relevant evidence, with a formal meeting being arranged for a later date.[34] She was subsequently unable to attend the formal meeting, having requested, and been granted, annual leave at the last minute relating to her most recent round of IVF treatment. Her experience reinforces the time-sensitive and inflexible nature of undergoing ART treatments, as well as the difficulties in evidencing treatment-related absences that are not limited to treatment appointments. Nevertheless, the meeting proceeded in her absence, and she was given a formal warning relating to her absences.[35] Sahota argued proceeding with the meeting, with the possibility of formal action being taken, amounted to less favourable treatment on the grounds of sex because she was undergoing IVF treatment.

The EAT adopted a narrow interpretation of the decision in *Mayr* and determined that it should be confined to its narrow focus on the period between follicular puncture and transfer.[36] While the EAT considered that a broader interpretation was possible, particularly in light of the CJEU's reference to the fact that IVF treatment, in general, 'directly affects only women,'[37] it reasoned that such an approach would be untenable. In particular, because such an approach could then be applied to all sex-specific illnesses or treatment.[38] However, given the approach adopted by AG Colomer and the focus on protecting procreation, a broader interpretation need not have been so all encompassing. Instead, it could have focused on the interconnection between the sex-specific treatment and childbearing capacity, with reference to the societal value of procreation, thus limiting the protected period to instances when individuals were undergoing treatment. The EAT also held that such an approach was consistent with the jurisprudence on pregnancy-related illness, which only affords special protection during pregnancy and the maternity leave period, with all other periods being comparable with other illnesses.[39] This reflects the concerns

---

33 *Ibid*, [18].
34 *Ibid*, [26].
35 *Ibid*, [30].
36 *Sahota* (n.32), [11]–[12].
37 *Mayr* (n.8), [50].
38 *Sahota* (n.32), [12].
39 *Ibid*, [7].

noted earlier regarding the *Mayr* decision.[40] The decision subsequently followed that in *Robinson*,[41] with absences for the purposes of undergoing IVF treatment being treated in the same way as any other periods of illness absence. Consequently, any hopes of extending the scope of sex discrimination protection in the UK to fully protect those undergoing ART treatments were dashed by the narrow interpretation adopted in this case.

These decisions show that while the CJEU has made some efforts to include those undergoing ART treatments within the scope of existing equality law frameworks, this has resulted in limited protection in very specific circumstances. Attempts, thus far, to redefine the scope of pregnancy protection have been the most challenging since it is inherently connected with traditional, biological and gestational aspects of pregnancy. Sex discrimination provisions have offered more opportunities, but the need for a comparator also poses significant problems for those undergoing treatment, unless analogies can be drawn with pregnancy and/or childbearing capacity, as well as broader equality law principles. This indicates that while both the protected characteristics of sex and pregnancy are relevant in this context, the boundaries of protection need to be reinterpreted and/ or redefined to more effectively include those undergoing ART treatments. Despite the limitations of the *Mayr* judgement, the importance placed on the value of procreation,[42] however this is achieved, remains notable and could still offer opportunities for broader interpretation in the future in the way envisaged here.

Childcare rights: commissioning mothers in surrogacy

In some respects, the experiences of commissioning parents in surrogacy can be distinguished from those undergoing ART treatments more generally in the UK. Specific rights to childcare leave have now been extended to commissioning parents, thus including them within the employment law framework. Nevertheless, this does not address the underlying question of whether they are included within the scope of equality law. Consequently, the jurisprudence on commissioning mothers and their attempts to extend the boundaries of equality law are equally relevant here. This section first examines the UK and CJEU decisions, focusing particularly on the Opinions delivered by the two AGs, which, although different, indicate that

---

40 Bell (n.25), 616; Kilpatrick (n.26), 190.
41 *Robinson* (n.1).
42 This, Fox argues, should be the starting point for equality law: (n.28), 6.

alternative interpretations of the boundaries of current protected character-istics are possible. The section then examines the UK extension of employ-ment rights, which again shows that change is possible in this context. These cases and legislative changes show that the closer it mirrors tradi-tional family models, the more likely it is to be accepted within the legal frameworks, which poses potential challenges for those undergoing ART treatments. However, it also highlights the willingness of the UK govern-ment to react in this context, which could have positive future implications for all those engaged in ART treatments.

The jurisprudence on commissioning mothers

Within both the UK and EU contexts, the right to maternity leave is inex-tricably linked with pregnancy, which poses practical and conceptual dif-ficulties for childcare rights of commissioning mothers in surrogacy. In the EU, Art.8 PWD grants a minimum of 14 continuous weeks' leave to work-ers as defined in Art.2 as pregnant workers, workers who have recently given birth or workers who are breastfeeding. This focuses primarily on gestational conditions and not biological or social motherhood.[43] The same is true for maternity leave in the UK. Reg.7 of the Maternity and Parental Leave etc Regulations 1999 (MPLR) entitles an employee to a total of 52 weeks' maternity leave. To be entitled to such leave the employee must satisfy the following conditions in Reg.4: she must notify her employer of her pregnancy by the end of the 15th week before her due date or, if that is not reasonably practicable, as soon as is; her expected due date; and when she intends to start leave. In both contexts, the focus is on the pregnant woman and not on the caring responsibilities thereafter, which, of course, often, but not always, coincide. This means that surrogates and women who place their children for adoption are equally entitled to the full mater-nity leave period irrespective of who cares for the child. The corollary of this is that commissioning mothers have either based their claims on other grounds or have attempted to broaden the scope of pregnancy.

   This issue was first raised in the UK case *Murphy v Slough Borough Council*,[44] in which the commissioning mother was refused paid child-care leave, instead being granted unpaid leave. She argued that the refusal amounted to disability discrimination, because her decision to use a

---

43 Eugenia Caracciolo Di Torella and Petra Foubert, 'Surrogacy, Pregnancy and Mater-nity Rights: A Missed Opportunity for a More Coherent Regime of Parental Rights in the EU' [2015] EL Rev 52.
44 [2005] ICR 721.

surrogate was related to a congenital heart condition which prevented her from carrying a pregnancy to term. The broader question of the interconnection between disability and infertility is explored further in Chapter 3; however, a few important points are noted here. Firstly, the case was argued on the grounds of disability rather than trying to reinterpret the definitions of those entitled to maternity leave. The latter approach would have immediately failed given the narrow qualifying conditions. Secondly, while the Employment Tribunal (ET) held that she had not been treated less favourably for a reason relating to her disability per s.5(1) of the Disability Discrimination Act 1995 (DDA),[45] this was overturned by the EAT[46] and not contested before the Court of Appeal (CoA).[47] The ET and EAT accepted that she was disabled,[48] in relation to her congenital heart condition,[49] but did not address the question of whether infertility per se was a disability. However, while the ET held that the difference in treatment was not related to her disability but her decision to use a surrogate,[50] this was overturned by the EAT, which accepted that there was a direct link between the two.[51] Thirdly, the case turned on whether the refusal could be justified per s.5(1).[52] The CoA accepted the reasoning of both tribunals that the refusal was justified on financial grounds.[53] It is notable that one of the issues relating to the financial impact was the unavailability of reimbursement by the state, unlike statutory maternity pay.[54] What is also significant is that the employer attempted to draw analogies with adopting parents, who would have similarly received unpaid leave. While efforts were made to assimilate the circumstances as closely as possible with other recognisable family forms, the lack of recognition of these relationships within the legislative framework had a significant impact on the availability of paid leave here.

This issue was subsequently considered by the CJEU, this time primarily through the lenses of pregnancy and sex discrimination. In both Case C-167/12 *CD v ST*[55] and Case C-363/12 *Z v A (Re Equal Treatment)*,[56] commissioning mothers sought access to paid childcare leave and in both

---

45 Now replaced by the EqA.
46 *Murphy v Slough Borough Council* [2004] ICR 1163 (EAT), [39].
47 *Ibid*, [6].
48 DDA, s.1 and Sch.1.
49 *Murphy* (n.46), [32].
50 *Ibid*, referring to [14] of the ET decision.
51 *Ibid*, [36]–[39].
52 *Ibid*, [9]–[32].
53 *Ibid*, [34]–[42].
54 *Ibid*, [35].
55 [2014] 3 CMLR 15.
56 *Ibid*, 20.

instances were refused. This was essentially on the grounds that they qualified for neither maternity nor adoption leave under national law. Having not been pregnant and not given birth, they were excluded from maternity leave. However, they were equally excluded from adoption leave because they had not adopted their children. It should be noted that in *CD*, the claimant was subsequently granted access to paid adoption leave, and in *Z*, the claimant was offered unpaid leave akin to that available to adopting parents.[57] However, in both instances, this was discretionary and not provided as a matter of right. This again shows some willingness to assimilate with other family forms, but in doing so, it also reinforces the value given to gestationally derived parenthood over alternative models, even where there is a similar biological connection.

Both cases were concerned with whether the refusals of paid leave amounted to sex discrimination, and both considered the scope of the PWD and the availability of the right to maternity leave therein.[58] *Z* raised the additional claim of disability discrimination because her reason for using a surrogate was that she had no uterus, although otherwise fertile, and so was unable to carry a pregnancy.[59] These cases reinforced the grounds argued in *Murphy* and presented another opportunity, this time for the CJEU, to consider the boundaries of the relevant legal frameworks. What is notable in both cases are the efforts made by the AGs, particular AG Kokott in *CD*, to reflect on and test the boundaries of EU equality law in this context. Unfortunately, the same was not true of the Grand Chamber, which adopted very narrow interpretations of the protected characteristics examined and their boundaries.

Firstly, in both cases, the commissioning mothers were not entitled to maternity leave under the PWD because they had not been pregnant.[60] This is despite the broad interpretation of the scope of the PWD offered by AG Kokott in *CD*. This went beyond the claimant's argument that breastfeeding mothers should be included within its scope, irrespective of whether they had been pregnant, to potentially include all commissioning mothers.[61] The justifications focused on the relationship between the mother and child and the rights of the child to be cared for.[62] Such an approach focuses on relationships of care and the needs of the child to be cared for as

---

57   *CD* (n.55), [AG19]; *Z* (n.56), [AG27], [42].
58   This was not explicitly raised in *Z*, but AG Wahl felt it was necessary to consider the application of the PWD here before addressing the discrimination claims [AG42].
59   *Z* (n.56), [AG24], [35].
60   *CD* (n.55), [35]–[43]; *Z* (n.56), [57]–[60].
61   *CD* (n.55), [AG53]–[AG63].
62   *Ibid*, [AG45]–[AG49].

opposed to focusing primarily on the biological/gestational connection.[63] Nevertheless, in a disappointingly narrow judgement, the CJEU rejected AG Kokott's teleological interpretation and instead adopted a more literal interpretation of the relevant provisions.[64] The Court disposed of the issues before it without any further consideration of whether the provisions could be interpreted more purposively. A similar approach was followed in *Z*.[65] In both cases, the commissioning mothers were easily excluded from the scope of the PWD because of the lack of gestational link.

Secondly, both cases turned to consider the sex discrimination claims, which also failed, primarily because commissioning mothers were not protected by the exception relating to pregnancy and using maternity leave.[66] Furthermore, the Court held that there was no less favourable treatment on the grounds of sex.[67] The symmetrical nature of protection here, in contrast with pregnancy discrimination, meant that the requirement for a comparator posed significant challenges. Both AGs considered different potential comparators, with both referring to male comparators in the first instance. AG Kokott specifically referred to male colleagues and AG Wahl to male parents.[68] While AG Wahl subsequently referred to male commissioning parents, the reference to 'or indeed otherwise' suggests that the comparator could equally be from the broader group.[69] This comparison is disappointing because fathers are not entitled to maternity leave, or any equivalent rights, at an EU level, and so this comparison was always going to fail.[70] Both AGs also considered alternative comparators, with AG Kokott suggesting that the appropriate comparison was with women who did not use surrogacy arrangements, although she conceded that this was not covered by the Equal Treatment Directive (ETD) since they do not differ in relation to their sex.[71] This would have offered a more meaningful comparison; if restricted to women who were pregnant, but this is also problematic because the comparators do not differ in relation to their sex.

63 Connie Healy, 'Once More with "Sympathy" but No Resolution for Intended Mothers: The EU, Ireland and the Surrogacy Dilemma', [2017] 39(4) JSWFL 504; Di Torella and Foubert (n.43), 66–68.
64 *CD* (n.55), [28]–[43].
65 *Z* (n.56), [57]–[60].
66 *CD* (n.55), [52]–[54]; *Z* (n.56), [57]–[60].
67 *CD* (n.55), [47]–[50]; *Z* (n.56), [52]–[55].
68 *CD* (n.55), [AG87]; *Z* (n.56), [AG63].
69 *Z* (n.56), [AG63].
70 Although certain rights are now contained in Directive 2019/1158 of the European Parliament and of the Council of 20 June 2019 on work-life balance for parents and carers and repealing Council Directive 2010/18/EU (WLBD).
71 *CD* (n.55), [AG87].

However, this comparison is also potentially problematic since Art.28 ETD permits an exception regarding the protection of women, particularly in relation to pregnancy, which allows more favourable treatment in this context. However, as is explored further in Chapter 4, this is not restricted to pregnancy and maternity, with the protection of women being the priority here. This poses the potential for a broader interpretation under this exception to include those undergoing ART treatments.

AG Wahl instead preferred the comparison with an adoptive parent,[72] but this is also problematic because again there were no equivalent EU rights for adoptive parents.[73] Despite the shortcomings of these approaches, it was clear that the AGs were aware of the unique circumstances of commissioning mothers and the difficulty of identifying an appropriate and meaningful comparator. Indeed, Di Torella and Foubert argue that AG Wahl's reasoning showed that there is an alternative approach to parenthood that could be considered here. Such an approach moves away from the biological/gestational paradigm and focuses more on childcare, irrespective of the ways in which the family was formed.[74] Such an approach is beneficial not only for commissioning mothers but also for fathers more generally, because it moves the focus on to the care of all children.[75] However, this is at odds with AG Kokott's opinion in which she states that the position of adopted children is distinguishable.[76] An approach which Di Torella and Foubert argue does not have the best interests of the child at its heart[77] and again has the potential to prize biological connection over relationships of care.

Nevertheless, the CJEU adopted a much narrower focus when considering an appropriate comparator. The Court in *Z* noted that the refusal of

72 *Z* (n.56), [AG64].
73 *Ibid*, [AG65]–[AG67]. This issue was referred to the national court to consider in light of the non-discrimination principle in Art.16 ETD, [AG67]. Now contained in the WLBD (n.70), Art.5.
74 Di Torella and Foubert (n.43), 62–63; Geert De Baere, 'Shall I Be Mother? The Prohibition on Sex Discrimination, the UN Disability Convention, and the Right to Surrogacy Leave under EU Law' [2015] CLJ 44, also argues that this approach is helpful, 47.
75 See also: Susanne Burri, 'Care in Family Relations: The Case of Surrogacy Leave' [2015] 17(2) EJLR 271, 279–80; Michèle Finck and Betül Kas, 'Surrogacy Leave as a Matter of EU Law: CD and Z' [2015] 52(1) CML Rev 281, 291–93; Petra Foubert, 'Child Care Leave 2.0 – Suggestions for the improvement of the EU Maternity and Parental Leave Directives from a Rights Perspective' [2017] 24(2) MJ 245, 261–63.
76 *CD* (n.55), [AG49].
77 Di Torella and Foubert (n.43), 63–64.

maternity leave only constitutes direct sex discrimination where the refusal related exclusively to one sex.[78] The Court in both cases focused on AG Wahl's comparison with a commissioning father and held that this did not amount to direct sex discrimination.[79] Notably, there is no reference to AG Wahl's preferred comparison of an adopting parent,[80] perhaps because there was no EU right to adoption leave and such a comparison would not have benefitted the mother either. Nevertheless, the result is that commissioning mothers are compared with commissioning fathers, who would not have been entitled to maternity leave in any event. A more appropriate approach would have been to deal with it as a special form of sex-specific protection, like pregnancy, without the need for a comparator. Alternatively, the Court could have recognised, as Cousins's argues, that women are more likely to be disadvantaged by the lack of paid surrogacy leave given the highly gendered nature of the use of childcare leaves and the possibility of breastfeeding. Consequently, refusing to extend paid leave to commissioning mothers would amount to indirect sex discrimination. This reflects the similar arguments made in relation to those undergoing ART treatments, which are also predominately sex-specific because of the connection with childbearing capacity, thus more likely to have detrimental implications for women. However, it is likely to be objectively justified given the diversity of societal and legislative approaches towards surrogacy within the EU and/ or based on financial considerations as in *Murphy*.[81]

The final issue raised was disability. While the English CoA in *Murphy* had previously held that refusal of maternity leave to a commissioning mother would not amount to disability-related discrimination, the CJEU had the opportunity to interpret the Framework Equality Directive (FWD)[82] in light of the UN Convention on Rights of Persons with Disabilities (CRPD),[83] which the EU confirmed in 2010.[84] Thus *Z* presented the opportunity for these issues to be interpreted anew through the lens of a different legal framework. While the CJEU noted that it must interpret

---

78 *Z* (n.56), [51].
79 *CD* (n.55), [47]; *Z* (n.57), [52].
80 *Z* (n.56), [AG64]. Adoption leave is discussed, but comparators are not considered, [61]–[65].
81 Mel Cousins, 'Surrogacy Leave and EU Law. Case C-167/12 CD v ST and Case C-363/12 Z v A Government Department' [2014] 21(3) MJ 476, 485.
82 Council Directive 2000/78/EC of 27 November 2000 establishing a general framework for equal treatment in employment and occupation.
83 Convention on the Rights of Persons with Disabilities 2007 [A/RES/61/106].
84 EU signed the Convention on 30 March 2007 and formally confirmed it on 23 December 2010.

EU law, including the FWD, consistently with the CRPD, it also noted that implemented was left to the discretion of contracting states.[85] The CJEU held that while it was possible that the claimant could have an impairment capable of constituting a disability under the CRPD, this was limited in the EU context by the requirement for it to have an impact on her 'full and effective participation in *professional* life' (emphasis added).[86] Consequently, for that reason, she was not considered disabled under the FWD.[87] The question of whether the CJEU applied the CRPD appropriately in its interpretation of the FWD is explored further in Chapter 3. Nevertheless, suffice to say the CJEU adopted a very narrow interpretation of the barriers to professional life and failed to acknowledge that the likely consequence of refusing paid leave to commissioning mothers is that they will forgo participation in professional life to care for their child. This is even more disappointing because the Court was invited to examine the claim from an intersectionality approach, considering the impact of both sex and disability together.[88] Nevertheless, the Court addressed each ground separately and did not consider the cumulative impact of these grounds and the disadvantage caused. As discussed further later and in Chapter 3, had such an approach been adopted, it may have been more effective at recognising the rights of commissioning mothers, as well as others involved in ART treatments.

Despite the criticisms of these decisions, many commentators also note that they were unsurprisingly cautious given the lack of consensus and the difficulty of addressing this within the existing equality law framework.[89] For instance, the legal bases for the actions in both cases were challenging to establish, which meant that it was always going to be difficult for the claims to succeed.[90] As De Baere suggests, the real reason *Z* failed was because her circumstances were outside the scope of the current legal framework.[91] This underscores a key issue here: that those involved in ART treatments do not easily fit within current equality law frameworks. AG Wahl's final remarks are also notable. Firstly, he noted the impossibility of the Court

85 *Z* (n.56), [AG114], [71]–[76], [88]–[90].
86 *Ibid*, [AG93]–[AG98].
87 *Ibid*, [77]–[82].
88 Raphaële Xenidis, 'Multiple Discrimination in EU Anti-Discrimination Law. Towards Redressing Complex Inequality?' in Uladzislau Belavusau and Kristin Henrard (eds), *EU Anti-Discrimination Law Beyond Gender* (Hart 2019) 69.
89 Burri (n.75), 278; Cousins (n.81), 484–85; Kate Ewing, 'Surrogacy: Beyond Equality?' [2014] 120(Apr) Emp LB 6, 7; Di Torella and Foubert (n.43).
90 Cousins (n.81), 484–85; Di Torella and Foubert (n.43), 62.
91 De Baere (n.74), 45.

to interpret the legislation more broadly to include the kind of protection sought here. Secondly, he raised the option of EU legislation to address this and recognise specific rights for commissioning parents, affording them the rights and protections sought here.[92] This again underscored an apparent willingness to extend protection further to recognise and reflect developments in society. In many ways, law is a driver of social and cultural change, but in this instance, AG Wahl recognised the need for law to respond to this gap. The same is true for all protections for those undergoing ART treatments.

These cases raise several important issues. Firstly, three main grounds of discrimination are argued in these cases, namely sex, pregnancy and disability. This aligns with the US experience, where women undergoing ART treatments have had some more success in interpreting and extending the same boundaries of equality law protection. Consequently, these three protected characteristics are the focus of analysis in Chapters 3 and 4. Secondly, most of the interpretations have failed to extend the boundaries of the protected characteristics, although efforts have been made to try to do so. This also underscores the difficulty of the CJEU being seen to be act as a legislator, particularly in an area which raises moral, ethical and societal issues that have not been resolved in member states,[93] although Di Torella and Foubert note that the CJEU has taken bold steps before to extend the scope of the protected characteristics and that this was another opportunity to do so, reflecting changing views on parenthood.[94] However, the underpinning ethical and moral issues relating to ART treatments, including the question of when life begins and the desire to exclusively protect the gestational and physiological aspects of childbearing, appear to have been key factors in the Court's reluctance here. Thirdly, an alternative approach is necessary to either redefine or broaden the boundaries of current protected characteristics. Such an approach needs to recognise and value the intersecting issues arising in cases involving those undergoing ART treatments, as opposed to addressing each ground in isolation. The cases also reinforce the Court's view that the role for doing this lies not with it but with the legislature,[95] either at the EU or a national level. This leads to the fourth point, which is that the first step may be introducing specific employment rights, in this instance for commissioning parents, enabling them to care for their children. Furthermore, it may be that solutions need to be found within member

---

92 *Z* (n.56), [AG120]–[AG121].
93 *Ibid*; Di Torella and Foubert (n.43), 66–67.
94 Di Torella and Foubert (n.43), 67–68.
95 *Z* (n.56), [AG121]; *Ibid*, 67.

states given the diversity of views across Europe[96] and the related challenge in reaching consensus on this matter. In the context of commissioning parents, the UK did just that by enacting specific employment-related rights.

The Children and Families Act 2014

Before the decision in *CD* was delivered, the UK government enacted the Children and Families Act 2014 (CFA), which extended a number of childcare-related employment rights to commissioning parents in surrogacy.[97] In the pre-natal period, this includes the right to attend two unpaid antenatal appointments with the surrogate.[98] While this enables commissioning parents to take time off to attend appointments, it fails to recognise that they have very different needs to traditional biological/gestational families. Not only will they have a similar vested interest in the progress of the pregnancy, but they also have a range of pre-conception needs that are not recognised in the legislation. Commissioning parents are likely to want to attend all key ART treatment appointments with the surrogate and may be required to attend certain appointments where they themselves are undergoing treatment. None of this is included within the current parameters of the legislation, which only begins following conception and, in effect, assumes that they will only want and need to attend the two key scans.[99] The fact that the leave is unpaid also suggests that they have a secondary role and status to that of gestational mothers and primary adoptive parents.[100] A more appropriate comparison would have been with adoptive parents, where one parent is entitled to attend five paid placement meetings prior to adoption.[101] While this is also limited, it would afford additional rights to paid leave and recognise a more involved role than is currently the case.

Following birth, commissioning parents are entitled to day-one rights to adoption leave.[102] The removal of the continuity requirements for adoptive parents is particularly significant for commissioning parents because it places them in the same position as gestational mothers using maternity leave.[103] However, the act adopts a traditional gestational family model

96 Cousins (n.81), 486; De Baere (n.74), 47.
97 As defined by HFEA 2008, ss.54–54A. CFA, pt 7, amending the Employment Rights Act 1996 (ERA).
98 ERA, ss.57ZE(7)(e)–(f).
99 Michelle Weldon-Johns, 'From Modern Workplaces to Modern Families – Re-envisioning the Work – Family Conflict' [2015] 37(4) JSWFL 395, 405–6.
100 *Ibid*, 406.
101 ERA, s.57ZJ.
102 Paternity and Adoption Leave Regulations 2002, SI2002/2788, Reg.15 as amended by Paternity and Adoption Leave (Amendment) Regulations 2014, SI2014/2112, Reg.7.
103 Weldon-Johns, (n.99), 404.

approach and fails to appreciate that this may not be necessary or appropriate for commissioning parents.[104] Only one is entitled to adoption leave,[105] with the other entitled to two weeks' paternity leave.[106] While both can instead utilise shared parental leave, providing they both satisfy the qualifying conditions and the parent entitled to adoption leave curtails it and instead utilises shared parental leave, this does not automatically enable them to share leave.[107] In addition, employer-provided shared parental leave pay is often not as generous as enhanced maternity (and possibly adoption) pay, and there is no requirement for employers to pay the same rate for both.[108] Thus, the available rights continue to reinforce traditional gender norms around childcare and prize gestational motherhood.

These amendments also highlight the stark differences between traditional biological/gestational families and those undergoing ART treatments. Despite being enacted in anticipation of the decisions in *CD* and *Z*, and addressing the issues raised therein, they were also enacted following the pre-conception rights decisions in *Mayr* and *Sahota* and do not offer those undergoing ART treatments any specific rights to leave or any greater protections against less favourable treatment and/or dismissal. In addition, the boundaries of equality law remain unchallenged, which also has particular consequences for those undergoing ART treatments. The examination of these cases and those relating to pre-conception rights demonstrates that the current approach to interpreting and defining the boundaries of existing equality law frameworks are inadequate and that a new theoretical and analytical framework is necessary. The literature on multidimensional and intersectional discrimination offers such an alternative analytical framework that would be more inclusive and better able to extend protection to those undergoing ART treatments.

A multidimensional, multiple or intersectional approach towards equality law?

An enduring characteristic within the literature on equality law has been calls to recognise the multidimensional, multiple and/or intersectional impact of discrimination in equality law frameworks. The extent to which the legislative frameworks have attempted to address this is discussed further

104 *Ibid*, 412.
105 ERA, ss.75A(8), 75B(a).
106 *Ibid*, s.80B.
107 *Ibid*, ss.75G–75H.
108 Joined cases: *Ali v Capita Customer Management Ltd* and *Chief Constable of Leicestershire Police v Hextall* [2019] EWCA Civ 900, 2019 WL 02256085. Jamie Atkinson, 'Shared Parental Leave in the UK: Can It Advance Gender Equality by Changing Fathers into Co-parents?' [2017] 13(3) Int JLC 356.

later, but it is first necessary to understand what these terms mean and the possible implications for equality law. Crenshaw first articulated the idea of intersectionality to raise awareness of the intersecting elements of disadvantage suffered by black women, which were not attributable solely to being a woman or being black, but instead on the intersecting and inseparable combination of characteristics.[109] Crenshaw's seminal views on intersectionality clearly demonstrate the limitations of a single-axis approach to discrimination law and the importance of recognising an individual's diverse and interconnected identities when developing legal responses to discriminatory treatment.

While intersectionality has its historical roots in black feminism and critical race studies,[110] it has been developed further by other scholars to include any instances where the disadvantage suffered is attributable to more than one protected characteristic.[111] Some of this scholarship refers to multiple or multidimensional discrimination rather than solely or specifically intersectional discrimination but equally encompasses this.[112] In doing so, this research identifies that despite the contested nature of the concept

---

109 Kimberle Crenshaw, 'Demarginalizing the intersection of Race and Sex: A Black Feminist Critique of Antidiscrimination Doctrine, Feminist Theory and Antiracist Politics' [1989] 1(Article 8) U Chi Legal F 137, 149.
110 Xenidis (n.88), 47.
111 Sarah Hannett, 'Equality at the Intersections: The Legislative and Judicial Failure to Tackle Multiple Discrimination' [2003] 23(1) OJLS 65; Manuela Tomei, 'Discrimination and Equality at Work: A Review of the Concepts' [2003] 142(2) Int'l Lab Rev 397; Mieke Verloo, 'Multiple Inequalities, Intersectionality and the European Union' [2006] 13(3) EJWS 211; Dagmar Schiek, 'Executive Summary' in Susanne Burri and Dagmar Schiek (eds), *Multiple Discrimination in EU Law: Opportunities for Legal Responses to Intersectional Gender Discrimination?* (European Network of Legal Experts in the Field of Gender Equality 2007) 4–5; Jess Bullock and Annick Masselot, 'Multiple Discrimination and Intersectional Disadvantages: Challenges and Opportunities in the European Union Legal Framework' [2012–2013] 19 Colum J Eur L 57; Maria Vittoria Onufrio, 'Intersectional Discrimination in the European Legal Systems. Toward a Common Solution?' [2014] 14(2) IJDL 126; Päivi Johanna Neuvonen, 'Inequality in Equality' in the European Union Equality Directives. A Friend or a Foe of More Systematized Relationships between the Protected Grounds?' [2015] 15(4) IJDL 222.
112 Dagmar Schiek, 'A New Framework on Equal Treatment of Persons in EC Law?' [2002] 8(2) Eur LJ 290; Dagmar Schiek, 'Broadening the Scope and the Norms of EU Gender Equality Law: Towards a Multidimensional Conception of Equality Law' [2005] 12(4) MJ 427; Dagmar Schiek and Victoria Chege (eds), *European Union Non-discrimination Law, Comparative Perspectives on Multidimensional Equality Law* (Routledge-Cavendish 2009); Victoria Chege, 'The European Union anti-discrimination directives and European Union Equality Law: The Case of Multidimensional Discrimination' [2012] 13(2) ERA Forum 275.

Conceptions of equality and the limitations 33

of equality,[113] including a diversity of appropriate responses to discriminatory treatment,[114] one of the main problems with equality law frameworks is the historical, and continuing, assumption that individuals have a singular determining characteristic that is the cause of any less favourable treatment. This makes it difficult to recognise and address multidimensional, multiple or intersectional discrimination in practice.[115]

Focusing on the notion of multidimensionality in the diversity of grounds covered by equality law and how they intersect and/or relate to each other leads to further diverging understandings on the nature of these interrelations. Distinctions are drawn between different conceptions of multiple discrimination,[116] which itself can be used as an umbrella term in this context.[117] At its most basic level, multiple discrimination can refer to the multiplicity of protected characteristics, without any additional reference to how they interact with each other.[118] In this sense, both UK and EU law embrace multiple discrimination because of the various protected characteristics included within the legislation. Multiple discrimination can also be viewed as 'sequential,' where the individual is discriminated against on one ground in one instance and then a different ground in another instance.[119] In this respect, the protected characteristics are still distinguishable and can be established separately. It can also mean 'additive' or 'compound' discrimination, reflecting that the individual is affected by discrimination based on two or more separate characteristics, each of which can be established independently. However, the discrimination experienced is exacerbated by

113 Amartya Sen, *Inequality Re-examined* (OUP 1992) ch.1. Sen argues that the notion of equality is faced with two diversities: 'the basic heterogeneity of human beings and the multiplicity of variables in terms of which equality can be judged', 1; Schiek, 'A New Framework' (n.112), 302–5; Schiek, 'Broadening the Scope' (n.112), 441–42.
114 Christopher McCrudden, *The New Concept of Equality* (ERA conference, Trier, 2–3 June 2003) <www.era-comm.eu/oldoku/Adiskri/02_Key_concepts/2003_McCrudden_EN.pdf> accessed 30 July 2019, 10–16.
115 Hannett (n.111), 66, 68–70.
116 Schiek, 'Broadening the Scope' (n.112), 461–62.
117 Schiek, 'Executive Summary' (n.111), 3–4. Although intersectional discrimination was used as an umbrella term by Timo Makkonen, 'Multiple, Compound and Intersectional Discrimination: Bringing the Experiences of the Most Marginalized to the Fore' (LLM thesis, Institute for Human Rights, Åbo Akademi University 2002) 10.
118 Schiek, 'Broadening the Scope' (n.112), 461.
119 Makkonen (n.117), 10–11; Sandra Fredman, 'Intersectional Discrimination in EU Gender Equality and Non-discrimination Law' (European Network of Legal Experts in Gender Equality and Non-discrimination, European Commission, 2016) 7, 27.

the addition of both grounds.[120] It can also be intersectional, reflecting the indivisibility of the different disadvantages relating to the combination of characteristics which is distinguishable from discrimination on any one of the separate grounds alone.[121] This is the most challenging to establish because the discrimination is not attributable to either ground alone but is the combination of prejudices that result in the detrimental treatment. These definitions reflect an increasingly complex view of individual identities and the impacts of less favourable treatment,[122] which cannot easily be defined or reflected in the boundaries of current individualised protected characteristics.

Many scholars argue that an intersectional approach is best suited to effectively address multidimensional discrimination. This is because it enables those hidden disadvantages to be disclosed, which can lead to better solutions for tackling them.[123] Bullock and Masselot identify three main limitations to the multiple discrimination approach, which they refer to as additive or compound discrimination.[124] Firstly, it presumes that all protected characteristics are the same and can be addressed in the same way in the legislation, despite this not being the case in practice. This is evident in the different classifications of current protected characteristics, which can be subcategorised as those that are ascriptions, those that are biologically based and those that are, in some respect, chosen.[125] However, these categories are not clear cut, and the same characteristic can be classified within different categories. Verloo argues that this diversity also shows that the categories can be unstable and contested,[126] reinforcing the problems with drawing the boundaries too narrowly in practice.

This mirrors some of the discussion around the categories of protected characteristics and how some are viewed as privileged over others.[127] For instance, in 2006, Verloo argued that the assumptions surrounding the

---

120 Makkonen (n.117), 11; Fredman (n.119), 7, 27.
121 Makkonen (n.117), 11–12; Hannett (n.111), 68; Schiek, 'Broadening the Scope' (n.112), 438–59, 462–64; Bullock and Masselot (n.111), 61–64.
122 Nitya Iyer, 'Categorical Denials: Equality Rights and the Shaping of Social Identity,' [1993] 19 Queen's LJ 179.
123 Bullock and Masselot (n.111), 64. A similar approach is favoured by Johanna Kantola and Kevät Nousiainen, 'Institutionalizing Intersectionality in Europe' [2009] 11(4) International Feminist Journal of Politics 459, 461–63.
124 Bullock and Masselot (n.111), 64–66.
125 Schiek, 'A New Framework' (n.112), 309–10; Tomei (n.111), 407–8 refers to the visibility of protected characteristics in a similar way. Verloo (n.111), 221 also draws similar distinctions (choice, visibility and ascription vs identification and probability and possibility of a change in identity and status in connection with inequalities).
126 Verloo (n.111), 221.
127 Neuvonen (n.111). See also Fredman (n.119), 30.

similarity of inequalities in the EU were inaccurate. With reference to various aspects of the social categories of sex, race/ethnicity, sexual orientation and class, Verloo showed that the different inequalities were dissimilar and were framed differently to make them relevant as political problems.[128] Consequently, she argued that this diversity should be reflected in the political strategies used to address them. In addition, protected characteristics can be over-broad and attempt to encompass all forms of disadvantage, even where they might be more appropriately attributed to multiple or intersectional grounds. Alternatively, they can be under-inclusive and exclude undesirable conduct because one of the reasons for the disadvantage suffered is not yet included within the equality law framework.[129] This is reflective of the experiences of those undergoing ART treatments where the equality law framework largely excludes undesirable conduct relating to undergoing treatment because it fails to fit neatly within the boundaries of the current frameworks.

Despite this, there has been a continuing focus on treating all protected characteristics in the same way, even though the legislation adopts different approaches to dealing with certain characteristics.[130] Neuvonen contends that such an approach fails to acknowledge what kind of equality underpins each protected characteristic. She acknowledges that the literature on substantive equality advocates for differential treatment in some instances to achieve equality. Consequently, treating different protected characteristics differently might be a more effective means of achieving equality in practice.[131] This reflects the argument that the protected characteristics are inherently different and related to different aspects of personal identity. Adopting an intersectional approach could ensure that this diversity is acknowledged and that the legal frameworks respond accordingly. This is particularly true for those undergoing ART treatments where an Aristotelian view of formal equality is inappropriate since it is difficult to assimilate this with traditional conception and/or male experiences of treatment. On the other hand, an asymmetrical substantive equality approach, as in disability or pregnancy discrimination, would be more appropriate.

Secondly, Bullock and Masselot argue that a multiple discrimination approach encourages competition between characteristics rather than

---

128 Verloo (n.111), 215–22.
129 Hannett (n.111), 72–79.
130 For instance, direct age discrimination can be justified, whereas this is not the case for the other grounds. Equally some characteristics adopt a symmetrical approach (sex, race, age), and others an asymmetrical approach (disability, pregnancy, marriage or civil partnership).
131 Neuvonen (n.111), 228–29.

coordination between disadvantaged groups, which creates a hierarchy of inequality. This encourages those wanting to advance or address the issues faced by certain groups to compete with one another for support and/or legislative reform, rather than coming together to support and address less favourable treatment against all disadvantaged groups. They argue that an intersectionality approach would instead highlight the ways in which the protected characteristics interact and develop more effective solutions.[132] This is particularly true in the discussions of those undergoing ART treatments in Chapters 3 and 4 where there is some reluctance to expand categories because of concerns about the misappropriation of the experiences of certain groups to benefit others. This is particularly evident in the context of using the disability rights discourse to include infertility as a disability. An intersectionality approach may reduce these concerns because the overarching objective is to reduce discrimination and unequal treatment for all disadvantaged groups.

Finally, Bullock and Masselot argue that multiple discrimination remains too narrow and can prevent solutions to tackling intersectionality to be developed. This is evident from the jurisprudence relating to ART treatments, which draw the boundaries of the protected characteristics too narrowly, even when presented with the opportunities to consider the issues through an intersectional lens. An intersectionality approach could enable the boundaries to be redrawn, allowing new solutions to be developed to respond to these new challenges.

However, intersectionality, particularly intersectionality theory, has also been criticised as being of little relevance to law,[133] too complex to offer solutions in practice and too rooted in Anglo-Saxon discourse to meaningfully relate to other areas.[134] There are also concerns that the groups identified using an intersectionality approach are increasingly split into smaller subgroups, with related challenges for establishing discrimination claims,[135] particularly when identifying a relevant comparator. Focusing on identities also creates the potential for stereotyping, with the assumption that these subgroups have a fixed identity,[136] which the example of those undergoing

---

132 Bullock and Masselot (n.111), 64–66.
133 Joanne Conaghan, 'Intersectionality and the Feminist Project in Law' in Emily Grabham, Davina Cooper, Jane Krishnadas and Didi Herman (eds), *Intersectionality and Beyond: Law, Power and the Politics of Location* (Routledge Cavendish 2009).
134 As noted in Dagmar Schiek and Anna Lawson, 'Introduction' in Dagmar Schiek and Anna Lawson (eds), *European Union Non-Discrimination Law and Intersectionality: Investigating the Triangle of Racial, Gender and Disability Discrimination* (Ashgate Publishing 2011) 2.
135 Fredman (n.119), 31.
136 *Ibid*, 32–33.

ART treatments shows is not the case. There is also the related challenge of a limited underpinning legal framework facilitating any kind of multidimensional and/or intersectional approach.

Multidimensional discrimination and the legal framework

As the overview of literature in this area indicates, the goal of attempting to embed multidimensional discrimination into legal frameworks has not been an easy task and is far from being achieved. There is much criticism, both in the EU and in the UK, regarding recognition of multidimensional discrimination within legal frameworks. In particular, scholars have argued that both have historically failed to provide an adequate legal basis for facilitating multidimensional discrimination claims.[137] EU developments in this area have equally failed to address this, instead adding new protected characteristics rather than recognising multiple or intersectional discrimination.[138] This is equally true in the UK, which has largely just implemented these changes into domestic law. Despite this, there is now some reference to multiple discrimination within both equality law frameworks, although they have not yet explicitly tackled intersectional discrimination,[139] and the references are largely non-binding.

In the EU, multiple discrimination is referred to in Recital 3 FWD and Recital 14 of the Race Discrimination Directive;[140] however, there are no specific legal provisions to support this within the Directives,[141] and the CJEU has not yet adopted an intersectional approach when interpreting cases raising such issues.[142] However, Fredman argues that Art.19 TFEU,[143] which provides the power to tackle discrimination on the named grounds,[144]

---

137 Hannett (n.111); Schiek, 'A New Framework' (n.112); Bullock and Masselot (n.111), 74–78.

138 Schiek, 'Broadening the Scope' (n.112), 438–40.

139 Dagmar Schiek and Jule Mulder, 'Intersectionality in EU Law: A Critical Re-appraisal' in Dagmar Schiek and Anna Lawson (eds), *European Union Non-Discrimination Law and Intersectionality: Investigating the Triangle of Racial, Gender and Disability Discrimination* (Ashgate Publishing 2011) 259–61.

140 Council Directive 2000/43/EC of 29 June 2000 implementing the principle of equal treatment between persons irrespective of racial or ethnic origin. Also referred to in: 2000/750/EC: Council Decision of 27 November 2000 establishing a Community action programme to combat discrimination (2001 to 2006), *Recitals 4–5*.

141 Chege (n.112); Onufrio (n.111); Fredman (n.119), 62–65.

142 Schiek, 'Executive Summary' (n.111), 7–9, 13–17; Schiek and Mulder (n.139), 262–63; Fredman (n.119), 71–79; Xenidis (n.88), 51–57, 60–74.

143 Consolidated version of the Treaty on the Functioning of the European Union 2012/C 326/01.

144 Sex, racial or ethnic origin, religion or belief, disability, age or sexual orientation.

suggests that there is no reason why claims cannot be brought on multiple grounds.[145] In addition, Art.21 of the Charter of Fundamental Rights of the EU (the Charter),[146] indicates that EU law must also be interpreted as non-discriminatory on any ground,[147] again supporting the possibility that multiple discrimination claims can be presented.[148] Although this approach would also be limiting because it would only facilitate multiple discrimination claims on dual grounds, indicating that an intersectionality approach would be better suited to addressing discrimination based on complex social identities.[149]

The UK position on multiple discrimination is more tenuous and likely to be even more so post-Brexit, especially given the intention to withdraw from the Charter.[150] The issue first arose in *Bahl v Law Society*,[151] which adopted an additive approach requiring each ground to be established separately.[152] Following criticism of this judgement, s.14 EqA was drafted to permit dual grounds to be raised in discrimination claims,[153] thus, in principle, allowing multiple discrimination claims to be raised. However, it was not brought into force at the time, and the subsequent Conservative–Liberal Democrat coalition government stated that they would not enact the provision either.[154] Thus, while the section remains in the statute, it has still not been enacted, and the UK position on multiple discrimination remains that adopted in *Bahl*. The loss of the interpretative potential of the Charter in this context also means that it is unlikely to be advanced in the future without positive steps being taken to meaningfully address multiple discrimination in practice. While frustratingly tentative steps have been taken to recognise that multidimensional discrimination exists, both legal frameworks continue to lag behind lived experiences. This reinforces why it is necessary to redefine the boundaries of discrimination law, not just in the context of those undergoing ART treatments but also more generally.

145 Fredman (n.119), 68.
146 Charter of Fundamental Rights of the European Union 2012/C 326/02.
147 ' . . . such as sex, race, colour, ethnic or social origin, genetic features, language, religion or belief, political or any other opinion, membership of a national minority, property, birth, disability, age or sexual orientation.'
148 Fredman (n.119), 68.
149 *Ibid*, 68–69.
150 European Union (Withdrawal) Act 2018, s.5(4).
151 [2004] EWCA Civ 1070 (Court of Appeal).
152 For a discussion of this judgement see: Aileen McColgan, 'Reconfiguring Discrimination Law' [2007] (SPR) PL 74, 80–81; Onufrio (n.111), 130–31.
153 Onufrio (n.111), 130–31.
154 HM Treasury and Department for Business Innovation and Skills, 'The Plan for Growth' (March 2011), 1.33, 2.51.

Setting the theoretical frame: ART treatments and intersectionality

Despite the current limitations within the legal frameworks, the goal of addressing multidimensional discrimination remains a key objective for the future development of equality law. Schiek argues that an intersectionality approach can be effective here but only where disadvantages are examined around the three nodes of 'race,' gender and disability.[155] This focus is particularly significant for those undergoing ART treatments, who primarily face disadvantage around the boundaries of gender and disability. Schiek originally presented this as an alternative interpretative model, primarily as a response to the concerns of increasing the number of protected characteristics in EU law and the related challenges for equality law.[156] These include creating unjustified hierarchies of protected characteristics[157] and redefining discrimination claims through the lenses of newer protected characteristics rather than acknowledging the underlying issues that may be rooted in more traditional ones, thus potentially diluting the underpinning purposes of equality law.[158] This reinforces why it is more effective to re-examine current characteristics to include those undergoing ART treatments. As is argued in Chapters 3 and 4, the disadvantage suffered is rooted in these traditional characteristics and requires similar legal responses.

The nodes model is presented as a more coherent way of restructuring equality law,[159] as well as being an interpretative device to influence judicial reasoning in the case law and future development of legislation.[160] Schiek later expanded on this as a way to re-organise EU discrimination law as a socio-legal field, meaning 'a social space established by social interaction on the basis of power struggles.'[161] This includes the interrelations between

---

155 Dagmar Schiek, 'Organizing EU Equality Law Around the Nodes of "Race", Gender and Disability' in Dagmar Schiek and Anna Lawson (eds), *European Union Non-discrimination Law and Intersectionality: Investigating the Triangle of Racial, Gender and Disability Discrimination* (Ashgate Publishing 2011); Dagmar Schiek, 'Intersectionality and the Notion of Disability in EU Discrimination Law' [2016] 53 CML Rev 35.
156 Schiek, 'Organizing EU Equality Law' (n.155), 11–18.
157 *Ibid*, 15–16.
158 *Ibid*, 16–18.
159 *Ibid*, 11.
160 *Ibid*, 19, 27. For a recent application of this see: Dagmar Schiek, 'On Uses, Mis-uses and Non-uses of Intersectionality before the Court of Justice (EU)' [2018] 18(2–3) IJDL 82.
161 Schiek, 'Intersectionality' (n.155), 51–52.

all key actors involved in discrimination law and policy as well as how this is shaped through all relevant legal sources, including the jurisprudence of the courts.[162] The potential of this model as an interpretative and analytical framework suggests that it could be beneficial for those undergoing ART treatments. This is further borne out in the discussion of the nodes themselves.

The model is constructed around three overlapping circles representing each node, each having a centre and an orbit, which allows for a multiplicity of grounds to be covered within them and appropriate responses to be provided.[163] The three nodes are chosen for three main reasons: firstly, because of the focus on these protected characteristics at an international level in international human rights instruments,[164] thus indicating their central importance to human dignity and recognition as fundamental human rights, and, secondly, because of the underpinning purposes of EU non-discrimination law, which Schiek argues can be reenvisaged as 'addressing social disadvantage within social reality.'[165] This focuses specifically on social disadvantages that are based on ascriptions because of their impact on the division of labour, within the labour market and in the home, and access to resources, all of which are equally relevant to those undergoing ART treatments. This is also underpinned by the rationales of individuation, enabling individuals to choose to move beyond the stereotypes that ascriptions prescribe to them, and respecting human dignity, by protecting and respecting difference.[166] Thirdly, these three nodes all can be classified in terms of being ascriptions, their significance to personal identity and the inherent problems with adopting a symmetrical approach to addressing inequality.[167] This is also reflective of the experiences of those undergoing ART treatments, both in terms of ascriptions regarding stereotypical and traditional views on childbearing and childbearing capacity and the limitations of adopting a symmetrical approach in this context. In addition, Schiek argues that the concept of nodes should allow intersectional discrimination to be conceptualised more easily because of the overlapping nature of the nodes, with issues closer to the centres being taken more seriously than those on the peripheries.[168]

162 *Ibid*, 52.
163 Schiek, 'Organizing EU Equality Law' (n.155), 18–19; Schiek, 'Intersectionality' (n.155), 52.
164 Schiek, 'Organizing EU Equality Law' (n.155), 19–20.
165 *Ibid*, 21.
166 *Ibid*.
167 *Ibid*, 22.
168 *Ibid*, 26.

Such an approach is useful in the context of those undergoing ART treatments particularly because of the focus on the intersections between gender and disability.[169] This is further reinforced in Schiek's descriptions of these nodes. The gender node encompasses the social structures that privilege those classified as male with respect to resources, labour market opportunities and personal autonomy. This includes challenging stereotypes relating to the division of labour and socially constructed expectations regarding biological, societal and caring roles. In addition, it includes the right to recognise, respect and accommodate physical difference, such as pregnancy and the ability to give birth.[170] Indeed, in later versions of the nodes models, Schiek specifically includes pregnancy within the orbit of the gender node.[171] In doing so, it recognises that there are some instances when women and men should be treated the same and others when an asymmetrical approach is more appropriate. This can equally be applied to those undergoing ART treatments. Using the nodes model, the socially constructed expectations around having a biological child and the role of the female partner in achieving this goal, as well as expectations around women undertaking primary caring roles, can all be recognised. In addition, the model should also include the need to recognise, respect and accommodate the different, inherently gendered, experiences of undergoing treatment. The potential of this model to include those undergoing ART treatments is arguably reinforced where gender intersects with the disability node, either as a situation requiring accommodation of difference or by conceptualising infertility as a disability.

At the centre of the disability node is 'any physical, psychological or mental difference resulting in diminished opportunities for participation in social life because those differences are not accommodated.'[172] Such an understanding adopts a social model of disability approach, explored further in Chapter 3, and is significant because the focus is not on the functional limitations of the individual but the socially constructed barriers. This could have significant implications for those undergoing ART treatments and the socially constructed barriers that are often faced when trying to combine

---

169 While 'race' may also be relevant, it has not been identified as an axis of concern in relation to employment rights, although it has in relation to access to treatment, which beyond the scope of this book: Arthur Greil, Julia McQuillan, and Kathleen Slauson-Blevins, 'The Social Construction of Infertility' [2011] 5(8) Sociology Compass 736.

170 Schiek, 'Organizing EU Equality Law' (n.155), 24.

171 Schiek, 'Intersectionality' (n.155), 52; Schiek, 'On Uses, Mis-uses' (n.160), 88.

172 Schiek, 'Organizing EU Equality Law' (n.155), 26.

this with paid work, as shown in the cases discussed earlier. Schiek also suggests that pregnancy may fall within the boundaries of the disability node where that intersects with gender, as a form of gender-related discrimination requiring the accommodating of difference.[173] Indeed, it is attributed to the disability node in later discussions of this model.[174] This again could include the experiences of women undergoing ART treatments, which similarly require accommodation of difference because of a physical difference that results in a diminished opportunity to participate in social life if not accommodated. Alternatively, it could specifically include infertility as a disability, since infertility has significant sex-specific consequences related to childbearing capacity, particularly in relation to the combination of work and treatment, that need to be accommodated. This suggests that adopting an intersectionality approach around these nodes could better accommodate the experiences of those undergoing ART treatments, irrespective of the reasons for doing so.

Schiek's approach is also relevant because it focuses on attempting to redefine the boundaries of equality law by expanding the concepts within the current legal frameworks. While Schiek's focus is analysing issues through these intersecting nodes, others have presented similar analytical approaches to broadening the scope of the current framework. For instance, a similar approach is referred to by Fredman as adopting a capacious interpretation of protected characteristics. This refers to broad interpretations of the boundaries and intersections within each characteristic, without the need to add new ones.[175] This is also referred to by Xenidis as the intracategorical route, focusing on modifying factors of disadvantage. Such an approach takes account of all aspects of an individual's identity, even within protected characteristics, and moves away from the focus on single grounds and the assumption that the other characteristics are privileged.[176] Like Schiek, Fredman argues that such an approach avoids the problems of multiplying grounds and/or limiting multiple discrimination claims to dual grounds only. However, Fredman does acknowledge that there can still be challenges, particularly in identifying the 'lead' ground upon which to base the discrimination claim. This is even more challenging when different characteristics have different legal frameworks, including exceptions and/or justifications.[177] Thus, making it difficult in practice to articulate

173 *Ibid.*
174 Schiek, 'Intersectionality' (n.155), 52; Schiek, 'On Uses, Mis-uses' (n.160), 88.
175 Fredman (n.119), 10, 69.
176 Xenidis (n.88), 67.
177 Fredman (n.119), 70.

and establish a valid, let alone successful, claim. Despite these potential shortcomings, these alternative analytical models indicate that broadening the scope of the current protected characteristics may be possible and desirable in certain instances to ensure appropriate protection within the current legislative frameworks.

Consequently, the current protected characteristics of sex, disability and pregnancy in the UK will be reinterpreted through the intersectional lenses of the gender and disability nodes presented by Schiek. Reflecting on Fredman's concerns regarding identifying leading characteristics, two alternative analytical frames are presented. Chapter 3 examines this from the lead perspective of disability intersecting with gender, and Chapter 4 from the lead perspectives of pregnancy and sex, which, for present purposes, fall within the gender node, intersecting with disability insofar as it is a difference requiring accommodation. In doing so, the value of this interpretative approach in practice is also examined.

Conclusion

This chapter has identified the various challenges within the current equality law frameworks, particularly for those undergoing ART treatments. Despite the potential for broader interpretations at times, the courts in both the UK and the EU have been unable or unwilling to extend the boundaries further to fully include those undergoing ART treatments. A review of the literature on multiple, multidimensional and intersectional discrimination indicates that an intersectionality approach offers the greatest potential to redefine the boundaries of protection. Schiek's intersecting nodes model is chosen because of its focus on gender and disability, which corresponds with the experiences of those undergoing ART treatments. Consequently, this model offers the opportunity to re-examine these experiences through these intersecting lenses as opposed to the single-axis approach that has been adopted thus far. This will enable conclusions to be drawn regarding whether there is the potential for the broader interpretations proposed here to be achieved in practice.

3 Conceiving a more social model of disability
Infertility as disability

Introduction

The question of whether infertility amounts to a disability has not been directly addressed in the UK or the EU. In those cases where disability has been raised, this has related to an underlying disability which has prevented an individual from carrying a pregnancy.[1] However, this question has been considered and accepted by courts in both the US and Canada. This chapter examines whether the UK definition of disability can similarly be interpreted more broadly to include infertility, and those undergoing ART treatments as a consequence. The chapter begins by setting the analytical frame, examining Schiek's disability node and models of disability. In doing so, the practical and conceptual limitations of the medical and social models of disability for those undergoing ART treatments are examined. Reference is made to the previous experience in Canada and the CJEU's limited application of the CRPD.[2] This underscores the potential of Schiek's intersecting nodes approach as an alternative analytical framework for expanding the boundaries to include those undergoing ART treatments. This potential is first explored through the lens of the US jurisprudence on the ADA,[3] which at times appears to indirectly endorse Schiek's intersectionality approach. This is then applied to the UK context where it is argued that a similar reinterpretation is possible.

---

1 *Murphy v Slough Borough Council* [2004] ICR 1163 (EAT) and [2005] ICR 721 (CoA); Case C-167/12 *CD v ST* [2014] 3 CMLR 15; Case C-363/12 *Z v A (Re Equal Treatment)* [2014] 3 CMLR 20.
2 Convention on the Rights of Persons with Disabilities 2007 [A/RES/61/106].
3 *Pub L No.101–336.*

Intersectionality, infertility and models of disability

As noted in Chapter 2, Schiek's intersectional nodes model can be used to facilitate an alternative interpretation of equality law. This chapter examines the experiences of those undergoing ART treatments primarily through the lens of disability intersecting with gender. Schiek argues that 'the definition of disability must encompass disabilities resulting from the interaction of impairment with other forms of discrimination.'[4] Thus, recognising the multiple and intersecting disadvantages that disabled people face and the need to embed this into the definition of disability itself. Schiek also grounds the disability node in similar terms to the social model of disability, as opposed to the medical model, which is more prevalent in legal definitions of disability. The medical model locates the disability in the individual caused by the impairment or illness, with some of its consequences relating to social disadvantage.[5] In doing so, it locates the disability firmly in the individual with the impairment. This approach focuses on a functional model of what the individual cannot do.[6] In doing so, it focuses on a medical understanding of whether the condition or impairment meets the appropriate standard to be considered a disability.

In contrast, the social model of disability has been referred to as ' "disability studies" proper' within the disability studies literature and is characterised by the argument that disability is located in society and its structures which create oppression, exclusion and inequality for those with impairments.[7] In doing so, it focuses on the way(s) in which disabled people are prevented from engaging fully in society. While impairments, when they are acknowledged, are understood in medical terms, it is argued that the disabilities experienced by disabled people are created by social structures.[8] This draws from the approach advocated by the Union of the Physically Impaired Against Segregation (UPIAS) in its 1974 Policy Statement.[9] These ideas were developed further by Oliver,

---

4 Dagmar Schiek, 'Intersectionality and the Notion of Disability in EU Discrimination Law' [2016] 53 CML Rev 35, 53.
5 Carol Thomas, 'How Is Disability Understood? An Examination of Sociological Approaches' [2004] 19(6) Disability & Society 569, 571.
6 Mike Oliver, 'Social Policy and Disability: Some Theoretical Issues' [1986] 1(1) Disability, Handicap & Society 5, 6; Colin Barnes and Geof Mercer, *Disability* (Polity 2003) 2–9, 25–29.
7 Thomas (n.5), 570–71.
8 Michael Oliver, *Understanding Disability: From Theory to Practice* (2nd edn, Palgrave Macmillan 2009) 45, 47–48.
9 <https://disability-studies.leeds.ac.uk/wp-content/uploads/sites/40/library/UPIAS-UPIAS.pdf> accessed 30 July 2019, paras.14–15.

whose seminal work articulated this as the social model of disability.[10] In doing so, Oliver noted that he was attempting to present an alternative to the individual (medical) model. In addition, it was an attempt to view the disabling barriers in a more holistic way rather than focusing on areas of disadvantage in isolation. Furthermore, he noted that he did not refute the significance or positive impact of individual interventions for disabled people. However, he argued that these were limited to individuals rather than providing more far-reaching benefits.[11] The social model instead offered a more practical approach by focusing on removing the structural barriers within society that persons with impairments (actual or perceived) face.[12]

However, the social model was not without criticism;[13] particularly relevant here was the critique that insufficient attention was paid to the intersections between gender and disability.[14] This was not unique to disability scholars, with it also being excluded from feminist movements.[15] This led to the emergence of literature on gender and disability, recognising the particular experiences and perspectives of disabled women.[16] This is equally reflected in the context of legal scholarship, which has increasingly

10 Michael Oliver, 'A New Model of the Social Work Role in Relation to Disability' in Jo Campling (ed), *The Handicapped Person: A New Perspective for Social Workers* (Radar 1981); Oliver (n.8).
11 Oliver (n.8), 45–46.
12 *Ibid*, 47.
13 As noted in: Vic Finkelstein, *A Personal Journey into Disability Politics* (Leeds University Centre for Disability Studies 2001) <https://disability-studies.leeds.ac.uk/wp-content/uploads/sites/40/library/finkelstein-presentn.pdf> accessed 30 July 2019, 6; Vic Finkelstein, *The Social Model of Disability Repossessed* (Manchester Coalition of Disabled People 2001) <https://disability-studies.leeds.ac.uk/wp-content/uploads/sites/40/library/finkelstein-soc-mod-repossessed.pdf> accessed 30 July 2019, 1; Carol Thomas, 'How Is Disability Understood? An Examination of Sociological Approaches' [2004] 19(6) Disability & Society 569, 573–75, 578–79; Oliver (n.8), 49; Mike Oliver, 'The Social Model of Disability: Thirty Years On' [2013] 28(7) Disability & Society 1024.
14 Jenny Morris, *Pride Against Prejudice* (The Women's Press 1991) 7–8; Barnes and Mercer (n.6), 58–59; Alison Sheldon, 'Women and Disability' in John Swain, Sally French, Colin Barnes and Carol Thomas (eds), *Disabling Barriers – Enabling Environments* (2nd edn, Sage 2004).
15 Nasa Begum, 'Disabled Women and the Feminist Agenda' [1992] 40 Feminist Review 70; Jenny Morris, 'Feminism and Disability' [1993] 43 Feminist Review 57.
16 Such as: Michelle Fine and Adrienne Asch, *Women with Disabilities: Essays in Psychology, Culture, and Politics* (Temple UP 1988); Morris (n.14); Carol Thomas, 'The Baby and the Bath Water: Disabled Women and Motherhood in Social Context' [1997] 19(5) Sociology of Health and Illness 622.

brought these intersections into focus.[17] This is evident in Schiek's intersecting nodes and her argument that the social model has failed to adequately include the experiences of disabled women, which can be better addressed by analysing them through an intersectional lens.[18] This is evident in the literature which has provided a voice for disabled women in relation to reproductive choice.[19] While there has been some discussion of access to fertility treatment,[20] it has not specifically addressed the question of whether infertility is a disability. As Schiek argues, focusing solely on the social model, as has been attempted thus far, insufficiently acknowledges the lived experiences of disabled people, particularly women. Nevertheless, the value of the social model is still recognised in Schiek's disability node. In this context, this is framed through the lens of a gendered analysis of the social model. In this way, while disability is presented as the central protected characteristic and conceptual node here, it is acknowledged that only by analysing it through the intersecting lens of gender can women's experiences of infertility be meaningfully understood and examined.

In doing so, it is acknowledged that those undergoing ART treatments are largely defined by these two intersecting characteristics, namely that they are women who are engaged in treatment because of their inability to conceive naturally. While the reasons are not exclusively fertility-related, this is the case for the majority of those undergoing treatment.[21]

17 Dagmar Schiek, 'Organizing EU Equality Law Around the Nodes of 'Race', Gender and Disability' in Dagmar Schiek and Anna Lawson (eds), *European Union Non-Discrimination Law and Intersectionality: Investigating the Triangle of Racial, Gender and Disability Discrimination* (Ashgate Publishing 2011); Schiek (n.4); Luísa Lourenço and Pekka Pohjankoski, 'Breaking Down Barriers? The Judicial Interpretation of "Disability" and "Reasonable Accommodation" in EU Anti-Discrimination Law' in Uladzislau Belavusau and Kristin Henrard (eds), *EU Anti-Discrimination Law Beyond Gender* (Hart 2019); Lisa Waddington, 'The Influence of the UN Convention on the Rights of Persons with Disabilities on EU Anti-Discrimination Law' in Belavusau and Henrard (n.17); Raphaële Xenidis, 'Multiple Discrimination in EU Anti-Discrimination Law. Towards Redressing Complex Inequality?' in Belavusau and Henrard (n.17).
18 Schiek (n.4), 48–49.
19 Anne Finger, *Past Due: A Story of Disability, Pregnancy and Birth* (Seal Press 1990); Thomas (n.16).
20 Leslie Francis, Anita Silvers and Brittany Badesch, 'Women with Disabilities: Ethics of Access and Accommodation for Infertility Care' [2019] Ethical Issues in Women's Healthcare: Practice and Policy; University of Utah College of Law Research Paper. <https://papers.ssrn.com/sol3/papers.cfm?abstract_id=3370556> accessed 18 July 2019.
21 Human Fertilisation and Embryology Authority, 'HEFA Fertility Treatment: Trends and Figures 2017' (HFEA 2019), 9, 13.

Their experiences are underpinned by stereotypical presumptions relating to 'normal' able-bodied female capabilities and roles, both in terms of biological expectations (i.e. the functional ability to physically bear a child) and societal expectations (i.e. the desire to want to do so). In these ways, their experiences reflect both the stereotypical and prejudiced assumptions underpinning disability and gender/sex discrimination. While the presumptions underpinning such stereotypical roles are unhelpful for women in general, particularly because of the related gendered assumptions regarding care, it is reflective of the experiences of women undergoing ART treatments.[22] Those undergoing treatment do so because of their specific desire to found a family and bear their own children. While it can be argued that this is a product of patriarchal views on women's roles,[23] it nevertheless remains the case that their desire to have their own biological children is a fundamental driver here. The inability to do so is reinforced by stigma based on functional normalcy as well as that attributable to traditional gendered roles. Consequently, it is apparent that only through analysing their experiences through these intersecting nodes can equality law effectively address their experiences and meaningfully consider whether they fall within the scope of equality law protection. This is evident in both the medical model approach adopted in the Canadian example and the purported social model approach adopted in the EU.

Infertility and the medical model of disability

As ARTs have advanced, so, too, have arguments in favour of the conceptualisation of infertility as a disability.[24] This has developed from the resulting medicalisation of infertility and the focus on medical treatments to remedy it. The medical model has been used to frame these arguments, which is at odds with the disability studies literature which has moved away from this model of disability.[25] However, in the Canadian context considered here,

22 Rachel Anne Fenton, D Jane, V Rees and Sue Heenan, ' "Shall I Be Mother?" ' Reproductive Autonomy, Feminism and the Human Fertilisation and Embryology Act 2008' in Jackie Jones, Anna Grear, Rachel Anne Fenton, Kim Stevenson (eds), *Gender, Sexualities and Law* (Routledge 2011) 242–44.
23 *Ibid.*
24 Judith Mosoff, 'Reproductive Technology and Disability: Searching for the Rights and Wrongs in Explanation' [1993] 16 Dal LJ 98. From a medical perspective: Abha Khetarpal and Satendra Singh, 'Infertility: Why Can't We Classify This Inability as Disability?' [2012] 5, 6 Australasian Medical Journal 334.
25 Daphne Gilbert and Diana Majury, 'Infertility and the Parameters of Discrimination Discourse' in Dianne Pothier and Richard Devlin (eds) *Critical Disability Theory: Essays in Philosophy, Politics, Policy and Law* (UBC Press 2006) 286.

this can be explained because they arose in the context of access to ART treatments under medical insurance plans. As Schiek notes, the conceptualisation of the medical model emerged not from a discrimination law perspective but in the context of legislation extending benefits and entitlements to disabled persons.[26] Consequently, in order to access such benefits, one would have to establish that he or she met the requisite standard of disability to be entitled to them. The same is true in this context, where the goal is achieving access to a benefit or entitlement rather than protection against discrimination.

Writing from a Canadian perspective, Mosoff examined and compared the distinct positions of disabled women and women who are, what she referred to as, 'reproductively disabled,'[27] who have used the disability rights discourse to gain access to ART treatments.[28] Using this discourse, and focusing particularly on the medical model, reproductively disabled women argued that they were entitled to access ARTs since they can be used to treat infertility.[29] Mosoff identified that such an approach meant three things: accepting the medical model, which meant arguing that treatment can fix or alleviate the impairment; framing the issue as one of allocation of medical resources; and drawing from the value of universal health care, which underpinned the Canadian health care system,[30] as is also the case in the UK with the National Health Service (NHS). What is notable about this is that reproductively disabled women were using the medical discourse, in contrast with the wider disability rights movement which had identified the inadequacies of this approach in advancing their rights.[31] This is particularly true for disabled women and how they constructed their rights, or lack thereof, to reproductive choice and freedom in very different terms.[32] This, in turn, led to dissatisfaction with the reference to the medical model here and with the broader arguments in favour of including infertility as a disability.[33]

This was reinforced in the Canadian context following the somewhat successful endorsement of infertility as a disability by the Nova Scotia CoA,

---

26 Schiek (n.4), 44.
27 Mosoff (n.24), 98–99.
28 *Ibid.* This was also recognised in a US study of women with fertility issues: Elizabeth A. Sternke and Kathleen Abrahamson, 'Perceptions of Women with Infertility on Stigma and Disability' [2015] 33(3) Sex Disability 3, especially 11–13.
29 Mosoff (n.24), 110–11, 118–19.
30 *Ibid*, 118.
31 *Ibid*, 119.
32 Thomas (n.16).
33 Gilbert and Majury (n.25).

in *Cameron v Nova Scotia (Attorney General)*.[34] The claimants argued that the exclusion of IVF and intra-cytoplasmic sperm injection from the medical insurance plan was a violation of s.15 of the Canadian Charter of Rights and Freedoms, on the grounds of their disability.[35] In considering this issue, the Court reasoned that it would have to adopt a broad approach, allowing alternative understandings of equality to be recognised.[36] Consequently, the majority decided that infertility was a physical disability and that the exclusion of treatment amounted to a distinction based on a protected personal characteristic,[37] although it also held that this was justified.[38]

The decision and reasoning were subsequently criticised by critical disability rights scholars Gilbert and Majury for reinforcing the medical model, which it did in several ways: firstly, by focusing on comparing those who are disabled with those who are not, thus focusing solely on capability;[39] secondly, by assuming that because infertility is a physiological condition, it is automatically a disability;[40] thirdly, by focusing on the historic and continuing stigma surrounding infertility and the vulnerability of those with fertility issues,[41] the decision and reasoning reinforced the stigma around infertility but without correctly addressing stigma as a defining characteristic of disability itself;[42] and, finally, by accepting the claimant's appropriation of the disability rights discourse, it reinforced and normalised this focus on the medical model, with related, negative, wider implications for disability rights, and disability rights discourse.[43]

The decision was further criticised for deciding that both claimants together were infertile and subsequently disabled.[44] Gilbert and Majury argued that this approach was problematic because it treated the female claimant as infertile when her partner had fertility issues.[45] In addition, the Court's reasoning focused on female infertility and treated both that and male infertility as if they were analogous.[46] While such an approach is problematic from a traditional equality perspective, it is perhaps understandable

34 [1999] NSJ No.297.
35 *Ibid*, [123].
36 *Ibid*, [129], [175].
37 *Ibid*, [145]–[176].
38 Under Canadian Charter of Rights and Freedoms, s.1. *Ibid*, [217]–[245].
39 Gilbert and Majury (n.25), 290–91.
40 *Ibid*, 292.
41 *Cameron* (n.34), [182]–[202].
42 Gilbert and Majury (n.25), 292–93.
43 *Ibid*, 285–86, 292–96; Mosoff (n.24), 112–13.
44 Reference is made to the 'infertile couple' throughout.
45 Gilbert and Majury (n.25), 286.
46 *Cameron* (n.34), [182]-[202]; Gilbert and Majury (n.25), 286, 294–95.

why it was adopted here. In this case, while the male partner had fertility issues, this had a direct impact on his wife's ability to become pregnant with a child that was biologically related to them both. His infertility, consequently, had a disabling impact on hers. This reflects what Shultz refers to as a form of social infertility.[47] Tomkowicz agreed that male infertility has an impact on the fertility of both partners but instead argues that each should be considered disabled in their own right.[48] However, Gilbert and Majury noted that treating both as infertile is problematic because it reinforces that women are responsible for the couple's capacity for childbearing, irrespective of who is infertile.[49] Nevertheless, given that only women can bear children, the reality is that they do bear the burdens of childbearing, including when this is affected by fertility issues, irrespective of their nature. While treating them in the same way makes it difficult to draw distinctions between who is disabled and who bears the social impact of the disability, adopting an encompassing understanding of infertility would enable more women to be protected from less favourable treatment and/ or dismissal while undergoing treatment.

While this attempt to access ART treatments focused on the medical model, others have argued that infertility fits into both the medical and social models of disability.[50] As the foregoing indicates, it fits into the medical model because infertility is often related to a physical impairment or genetic abnormality and/or is related to an underlying condition or disability. Consequently, medical treatment is often required to try to remedy the impairment. In doing so, it reproduces Gilbert and Majury's argument criticising the presumption that the presence of a physical impairment automatically amounts to a disability, an argument that is similarly raised in the US context, as discussed later. However, it is argued that it also fits into the social model because of societal pressures to reproduce which, Khetarpal and Singh argue, created the medicalisation of infertility in the first place. They argue that the pressure and the social stigma of infertility are apparent in many cultures and religions[51] and reinforce the kind of social oppression envisaged in the social model of disability. A small-scale study of US

---

47 Marjorie Maguire Shultz, 'Reproductive Technology and Intent-Based Parenthood: An Opportunity for Gender Neutrality' [1990] Wis L Rev 297, 314–16.
48 Sandra M. Tomkowicz, 'The Disabling Effects of Infertility: Fertile Grounds for Accommodating Infertile Couples under the Americans with Disabilities Act' [1995] 46 Syracuse L Rev 1051.
49 Gilbert and Majury (n.25), 287–88; Sternke and Abrahamson (n.28), 5.
50 Khetarpal and Singh (n.24), 336–37.
51 For an overview see: Lisa D. Powell, 'The Infertile Womb of God: Ableism in Feminist Doctrine of God' [2015] 65(1) Cross Currents 116.

women with infertility issues showed that they considered that the stigma surrounding infertility could be overcome by classifying it as a disability.[52] Indeed, both of these themes are evident in the reasoning of the Canadian Court in reaching its decision.[53] Nevertheless, Gilbert and Majury argue that infertility does not meet the requirements of the social model. While it may amount to an impairment, they argue that there are insufficient stigma, societal barriers and historical disadvantage for it to be considered a disability. Even if there was, the response sought, access to treatment, would not necessarily be the one the social model would provide, which is more likely to be to address the societal barriers and response to infertility rather than resorting to treatment to overcome it.[54]

Nevertheless, it is important to remember that the underpinning objective in the Canadian context was to gain access to treatments, as opposed to recognising the right to protection against discrimination.[55] In the UK context, service users are already covered by the EqA.[56] While decisions on treatment are at the discretion of medical practitioners,[57] this is subject to ensuring that decisions are not discriminatory on the grounds of any protected characteristics, including disability. Access to fertility services is also covered by Article 25(a) of the CRPD, which includes access to sexual and reproductive health services and/or programmes. This does not specifically refer to infertility treatment but could be interpreted as falling within its scope and would require that disabled persons have the same access to such services. While access to treatment and disability is worthy of further exploration, it is outside the scope of this text.[58] It is instead the position of those undergoing ART treatments, and their protection against employment-related discrimination while doing so, that is under consideration here. Given this change of focus, it is easier to see how a social model of disability would be better suited to include infertility as a disability. In doing so, the focus is on the social structures, in this case employment and

---

52 Sternke and Abrahamson (n.28), 11–14.
53 *Cameron* (n.34), [182]–[202].
54 Gilbert and Majury (n.25), 296–97.
55 *Ibid*, 296, suggest that infertility is only likely to be classified as disability in the context of access to funding.
56 EqA, ss.28–29.
57 Marie Fox, 'The Human Fertilisation and Embryology Act 2008: Tinkering at the Margins' [2009] 17 (3) Fem LS 333, 337; Rachel Anne Fenton, Susan Heenan and Jane Rees, 'Finally Fit for Purpose? The Human Fertilization and Embryology Act 2008' [2010] 32(3) JSWFL 275, 278.
58 See further: Fenton, Rees and Heenan (n.22); Atina Krajewska, 'Access of Single Women to Fertility Treatment: A Case of Incidental Discrimination?' [2015] 23(4) Med L Rev 620; Francis, Silvers, and Badesch (n.20).

equality law as well as employment practices, that have a disabling impact on the ability of women to undergo ART treatments while remaining in work. However, the CJEU decisions purporting to adopt a social model have fallen short here.

Infertility and the limitations of the EU interpretation of the social model of disability

Disability is not defined in the EU FWD,[59] which Quinn and Flynn argue is consistent with a civil rights perspective on disability.[60] The boundaries of protection have instead developed through the jurisprudence of the CJEU. The definition was first limited in C-13/05 *Chacón Navas v Eurest Colectividades SA*,[61] reflecting the medical model.[62] The CJEU followed AG Geelhoed's analysis of Art.13 EC Treaty, now Art.19 TFEU,[63] the FWD and his acknowledgement of the challenges of adopting anything more than a restrained interpretation of their scope.[64] Nevertheless, it has, in principle, expanded following the EU's confirmation of the CRPD, and the requirement to interpret EU law consistently with it.[65] Before examining the limitations of the CJEU approach, it is useful to first consider the relevant provisions of the CRPD.

The CRPD was a watershed moment in the disability rights movement. It marked a move towards a rights-based approach rather than one based on social welfare.[66] In doing so, it was heavily influenced by the social

---

59 Council Directive 2000/78/EC of 27 November 2000 establishing a general framework for equal treatment in employment and occupation, Arts.1, 5.

60 Gerard Quinn and Eilionóir Flynn, 'Transatlantic Borrowings: The Past and Future of EU Non-discrimination Law and Policy on the Ground of Disability' [2012] 60(1) Am J Comp L 23, 40–41.

61 [2006] ECR I-6467.

62 *Ibid*, [AG76] and [43]. For critique of the decision see: David L Hoskings, 'A High Bar for Disability Rights' [2007] 36(2) ILJ 228; Silvia Favalli and Delia Ferri, 'Tracing the Boundaries between Disability and Sickness in the European Union: Squaring the Circle?' [2016] 23 EJHL 5, 22–25; Lisa Waddington, 'Saying All the Right Things and Still Getting It Wrong: The Court of Justice's Definition of Disability and Non-Discrimination Law' [2015] 22(4) MJ 576, 578–79.

63 Consolidated version of the Treaty on the Functioning of the European Union 2012/C 326/01.

64 *Chacón Navas* (n.61), [AG46]–[AG56], [44]–[47].

65 Under Art.216(2) TFEU all international agreements, including the CRPD, are binding on member states and institutions. Secondary legislation must be interpreted consistently with this, as far as possible.

66 Rosemary Kayess and Phillip French, 'Out of Darkness into Light? Introducing the Convention on the Rights of Persons with Disabilities' [2008] 8(1) HRL Rev 1, 2–4.

model of disability,[67] as well as the US civil rights model,[68] although it has been argued that it now embodies a human rights model.[69] However, given the challenges around adopting an acceptable definition of disability,[70] the convention does not officially define disability in Art.2. Instead, persons with disabilities are described in Art.1 in broad terms as

> those who have long-term physical, mental, intellectual or sensory impairments which in interaction with various barriers may hinder their full and effective participation in society on an equal basis with others.

This reinforces preamble para.5, which recognises

> that disability is an evolving concept and . . . results from the interaction between persons with impairments and attitudinal and environmental barriers that hinders their full and effective participation in society on an equal basis with others.

This understanding of persons with disabilities is in many ways very broad and encompassing, allowing a wide range of individuals to fall within its scope. Although it does require that the impairment be long term, thus excluding temporary conditions and possibly also those where symptoms fluctuate.[71] Nevertheless, the focus is on the social barriers rather than the individual with the impairment. Despite this, some argue that it does not fully embrace the social model.[72] For instance, Kayess and French argue that the Convention fails to appropriately understand the connection between impairment and disability, suggesting that the person is only disabled once they are discriminated against.[73] However, it is possible to interpret Art.1 more broadly. Indeed, Lawson argues that the wording suggests that there is no requirement that the impairment *actually* hinders engagement in society, just that it *may* have this effect.[74] This is significant because not only does it recognise that the individual with the impairment is not the

---

67 Waddington (n.17), 341.
68 Quinn and Flynn (n.60), 34–39.
69 Theresia Degener, 'Disability in a Human Rights Context' [2016] 5(3) Laws 35.
70 Kayess and French (n.66), 23.
71 *Ibid*, 24.
72 Schiek (n.4), 47.
73 Kayess and French (n.66), 21–22.
74 Anna Lawson, 'Disability and Employment in the Equality Act 2010: Opportunities Seized, Lost and Generated' [2011] 40(4) ILJ 359, 363–64.

cause of the disability or disadvantage, but it also ensures that they do not have to prove that their participation in society has actually been hindered, just that it could be. This adopts a more inclusive understanding of disability and the lived experiences of disabled people. This may be particularly significant for those undergoing ART treatments who can otherwise engage in employment but may be prevented from combining work while undergoing treatment because of the disabling barrier of the lack of legal framework enabling them to do so.

The potential for developing EU disability law through implementing the CRPD has long been recognised.[75] However, while the jurisprudence following the decision in Joined Cases C-335/11 and C-337/11 *HK Danmark (Ring and Skoube Werge)* appears to endorse this model,[76] it is constrained in practice by the scope of the FWD, which is limited to employment and occupation. Thus, while the CJEU refers to the language of the social model of disability, it continues to reinforce the medical model in practice.[77] This is evident in *Z*, which is the only case involving disability and ART treatments decided by the CJEU. While the question of whether infertility is a disability was not directly raised, given the nature of her condition, absence of a uterus but otherwise fertile, the question of whether she was disabled under the legislation is closely linked to this consideration. At first glance, and by adopting a social model approach, it seems possible that infertility could be interpreted as within the scope of disability. Indeed, AG Wahl accepted that Z could be disabled under the broad understanding of disability in the CRPD since her physical impairment may 'hinder [her] full and effective participation in society.'[78] This reinforced the potential of the social model in accepting infertility as a disability and of the Convention facilitating such a broad interpretation of the boundaries of disability protection. However, given the more limited scope of EU law, it did not amount to a disability here, because it did not impair her full and effective

---

75 Lisa Waddington, 'Future Prospects for EU Equality Law: Lessons to Be Learnt from the Proposed Equal Treatment Directive' [2011] 36(2) EL Rev 163, 173–79.

76 EU:C:2013:222, [2013] 3 CMLR 21; *Z* (n.1); C-356/12 *Glatzel v Freistaat Bayern* EU:C:2014:350; [2014] 3 CMLR 52 (although not decided under the FWD); Case C-354/13 *Fag og Arbejde (FOA) v Kommunernes Landsforening (KL)* (Kaltoft) EU:C:2014:2463; [2015] 2 CMLR 19. See further: Favalli and Ferri (n.62), 28–34; Waddington (n.62), 579–83; Sandra Fredman, 'Intersectional Discrimination in EU Gender Equality and Non-discrimination Law' (European Network of Legal Experts in Gender Equality and Non-discrimination, European Commission 2016) 49–50, 78–79.

77 Waddington (n.62), 583–89; Schiek (n.4), 54–59; Waddington (n.17), 344–50.

78 *Z* (n.1), [AG93].

participation in professional life.[79] In delivering his Opinion, AG Wahl indicates that the limitations were within the scope of the FWD, which prevented the broader interpretation that the CRPD would afford from being implemented here:

> As profoundly unjust as the inability to have a child by conventional means may be perceived to be by a person who wishes to have a child of his or her own, I cannot interpret the existing EU legislative framework as covering situations which are not linked to the capacity of the person concerned to work.[80]

This approach was similarly adopted by the CJEU.[81] Consequently, the scope of the legislation was, in fact, the barrier preventing protection from being extended here. Schiek argues that this approach focused on the medical condition rather than the societal barriers that create disability, thus again adopting a medical approach despite referring to the language of the social model in the judgement.[82] This underscores the challenges of implementing the social model in practice and the consequent recourse to the medical model to fill the gaps.[83] In doing so, not only did the Court fundamentally misapply the CRPD by interpreting the definition too narrowly and thus contrary to the Convention,[84] but it also misunderstands the impact on professional life. Indeed, as several scholars argue, her ability to access employment-related rights concerns 'employment and working conditions' as well as potentially also including 'pay' per Art.3(1)(c) FWD. Thus, Z's ability to access these rights is indirectly limited by her disability and should come within the scope of the FWD.[85] The specific barrier being the absence of employment rights to childcare-related leave.[86] Waddington argues that the focus on professional life means that even if discrimination or exclusion is experienced in the context of professional life, it will

79   *Ibid*, [AG95].
80   *Ibid*, [AG97].
81   *Ibid*, [79]–[82].
82   Waddington (n.62), 585; Schiek (n.4), 56.
83   Theresia Degener, 'The Definition of Disability in German and Foreign Discrimination Law' [2006] 26(2) Disability Studies Quarterly, 2(a); Schiek (n.4), 47.
84   Eugenia Caracciolo Di Torella and Petra Foubert, 'Surrogacy, Pregnancy and Maternity Rights: A Missed Opportunity for a More Coherent Regime of Parental Rights in the EU' [2015] EL Rev 52, 66.
85   Mel Cousins, 'Surrogacy Leave and EU law. Case C-167/12 CD v ST and Case C-363/12 Z v A Government Department' [2014] 21(3) MJ 476, 486; Di Torella and Foubert (n.83), 65–66; Waddington (n.62), 585; Waddington (n.17), 346–47.
86   Waddington (n.62), 585; Waddington (n.17), 346–47.

not be covered by the FWD.[87] This was the case for Z and reinforces the challenges associated with framing discrimination in such narrow terms. In doing so, it fails to acknowledge the socially created barriers to engagement in professional life in instances where the impairment does not directly prevent or hinder someone from working.[88] This contrasts notably with the US 7th CoA decision in *McWright v Alexander*, in which the Court had no difficulty in determining that access to childcare leave was inherently related to work and within the scope of protection there.[89]

However, even when adopting a gendered perspective on disability, Schiek concluded that the decision in Z would have been the same because the inability to bear children does not disadvantage labour market engagement. In supporting this point, Schiek compares it with the position of men and their inability to bear children, which is often attributed to their stronger labour market position. Consequently, Schiek argues that her impairment would not be an effective basis for establishing disability.[90] However, Schiek's approach here fails to acknowledge, as the scholars discussed earlier do, the inherent impact on labour market engagement that results from the absence of rights and protection. Furthermore, comparisons with men are inappropriate. It is not the inability to bear children in the abstract that is at issue here. In the context of commissioning mothers, it is the interconnection between childbearing capacity and gendered, gestationally derived childcare rights that is the issue there. For those undergoing ART treatments, it is the interconnection between childbearing capacity and the sex-specific experiences of treatment that is the key consideration. In addition, others have argued that adopting an intersectional analysis could extend the scope of protection here. For instance, Xenidis argues that adopting an inter-categorical intersectional analysis of the combined effects of both disability and gender would have recognised the discriminatory disadvantage experienced here.[91] In particular 'an inter-categorical approach considering the co-exclusionary effects of disability and gender on access to motherhood would have helped to overcome a strictly biological conception of motherhood.'[92] Such an approach also focuses more on childbearing capacity and the consequences for women involved in ART treatments, which is arguably more appropriate here.

87 Waddington (n.17), 349.
88 *Ibid*, 349–50.
89 982 F.2d.222 (7th Cir 1992), [20].
90 Schiek (n.4), 60.
91 Xenidis (n.17), 69.
92 *Ibid*.

Furthermore, AG Wahl's opinion suggests a potential willingness to include infertility as a disability, at least within the scope of the CRPD. If this is the case, it further suggests that both the UK and EU definitions of disability could, and should, be capable of being interpreted more broadly to redefine the boundaries of disability here. This indicates that the influence of the CRPD has not yet been fully realised and underscores that the way in which it has been applied in the EU means that the person must establish that they are actually disabled before they can assert their rights to protection.[93] This echoes the concern raised by Kayess and French that was noted earlier. Schiek argues that the threshold should instead be exclusions stemming from the ascription of disability, since unequal treatment most often stems from this.[94] Such an approach would be much more inclusive and in-line with the goals of the CRPD and also consistent with the US approach discussed later.

Furthermore, Schiek argues that the distinction between the medical and social models is not the appropriate starting point for developing an EU definition of disability, particularly from an intersectional perspective.[95] With reference to the intersecting nodes model, particularly disability and gender, Schiek argues that these decisions underscore that the definition of disability fails to adequately include those conditions that women are more susceptible to.[96] In particular, there is a focus on physical and visible impairments, which also inherently excludes infertility. Thus, reinforcing the need for an alternative interpretative approach to both better recognise the experiences of disabled women and to ensure effective implementation of the CRPD.

Reinterpreting disability: adopting an intersectionality approach

The foregoing has demonstrated the challenges of attempting to interpret the boundaries of disability protection by focusing on medical or social models of disability alone. This section turns to consider the potential of the intersectionality approach, examining these experiences through the intersecting lenses of disability and gender. The US experience is examined first as this potential is demonstrated in the jurisprudence. It is also a useful comparator because of its progressive approach in the disability context,[97] which was drawn from in drafting the CRPD.

---

93 Schiek (n.4), 58.
94 *Ibid.*
95 *Ibid*, 44.
96 Fredman (n.76), 77–79; *Ibid*, 59–61.
97 Nick Wenbourne, 'Disabled Meanings: A Comparison of the Definitions of Disability in the British Disability Discrimination Act of 1995 and the Americans with

Infertility as disability: the ADA

The ADA was enacted to address gaps in the existing legal framework and provide comprehensive protection against discrimination, as well as promote equal opportunities for disabled persons.[98] Consequently, the act includes both a functional individualised definition of disability and protection against the social construction of disability, based on perceptions and stereotypes rather than actual functional abilities.[99] Disability was originally defined in Sec.12102.Definitions as

(2)(A) a physical or mental impairment that substantially limits one or more of the major life activities; (B) a record of such an impairment; or (C) being regarded as having such impairment.

Such an approach is referred to as a sociopolitical or civil rights model and is akin to the social model of disability because it focuses on the external socially constructed barriers that disabled persons face.[100] However, Finkelstein cautions that civil rights movements are about securing legal rights, which are individualistic in nature and do not necessarily reflect the social model of disability. While the social model does support civil rights, it is not reliant on them. Instead, he argues that the US legislation is not underpinned by a radical social model of disability.[101] While this is evident in the framework of the legislation which adopts a functional medical model approach to defining disability as followed in the UK, the inclusion of protections based on ascriptions of disability suggests that it includes more of a hybrid socio-medical model approach.[102]

Despite concerns over the uncertainty that a vague definition of disability would produce, the definition was nevertheless expressed in broad

---

Disabilities Act of 1990' [1999] 23(1) Hastings Int'l & Comp L Rev 149; Quinn and Flynn (n.60); Jeffery Miller, 'The European Disability Rights Revolution' [2019] 44(1) EL Rev 67.

98 Lowell P. Jr. Weicker, 'Historical Background of the Americans with Disabilities Act' [1991] 64 Temp LR 387, 390.

99 Wendy Wilkinson, 'Judicially Crafted Barriers to Bringing Suit under the Americans with Disabilities Act [1997] 38 S Tex L Rev 907, 909–11; Richard K. Scotch, 'Models of Disability and the Americans with Disabilities Act' [2000] 21 Berkeley J Emp & Lab L 213, 217–18.

100 Wilkinson (n.99), 915; Scotch (n.98), 214–17; Andrew I. Batavia and Kay Schriner, 'The Americans with Disabilities Act as Engine of Social Change: Models of Disability and the Potential of a Civil Rights Approach' [2001] 29(4) Policy Studies Journal 690, 691–92; Quinn and Flynn (n.60), 29, 31–34.

101 Finkelstein, 'The Social Model' (n.13).

102 Batavia and Schriner (n.100), 692.

terms, allowing it to be expanded as conditions and disorders developed in the future.[103] Like the UK definition of disability, it contains several elements. Firstly, there is a physical or mental impairment. Secondly, it limits a major life activity. Thirdly, that the limit is substantial. Physical or mental impairments and major life activities were not further defined within the legislation. However, the Equal Employment Opportunities Commission (EEOC) interpretative guidance included reproductive systems within its definition of physical impairments, and it was also noted that physical impairments must be physiological disorders.[104] *Major life activity* was defined in the guidance as 'those basic activities that the average person can perform with little or no difficulty.'[105] *Substantially limits* was defined as meaning that the disabled person is less able to perform the activity than the average person. That is determined from the point of view of the disabled person and the nature and severity of the impairment, the (expected) duration and the (expected) permanent or long-term impact of the impairment, which are all considered in determining if it substantially limits the major life activity in question.[106] These broad definitions led some to argue that infertility falls within the scope of the legislation.

Challenging the boundaries of disability

There are two opposing lines of authority in the US both including and excluding infertility as a disability from the scope of ADA protection. These decisions primarily turned on the question of whether reproduction was a 'major life activity' and whether infertility substantially limits it, with it generally being accepted that infertility is a physical impairment. The first case addressing this was *Pacourek v Inland Steel Company*,[107] in which the plaintiff was dismissed following absences relating to undergoing ART treatments, which the employer was aware of and agreed to support.[108] Pacourek raised several claims, but under the ADA, she claimed that her condition (esphofical reflux which prevented her conceiving naturally) amounted to a

103 Deborah K. Dallmann, 'The Lay View of What "Disability" Means Must Give Way to What Congress Says It Means: Infertility As a "Disability" Under the Americans with Disabilities Act' [1996] 38(1) Wm & Mary L Rev 371, 373.
104 EEOC, Regulations to Implement the Equal Employment Provisions of the Americans with Disabilities Act, 29 CFR (29 CFR), §1630.2(h)(1)-(2), discussed *ibid*, 381–82.
105 *Ibid*, §1630.2(i), discussed *ibid*, 382.
106 *Ibid*, §1630.2(j)(1)(i)–(ii) and §1630.2(j)(2), discussed *ibid*, 383–84.
107 858 F.Supp.1393 (ND Ill 1994).
108 *Ibid*, 1396–97.

physical impairment, substantially limiting reproduction, which she argued was a major life activity. Consequently, the employer's application of the sick leave policy amounted to disability discrimination and was to her detriment since she was dismissed. Her employers contended that infertility was not a disability under the ADA.[109]

The case first came before the District Court, which addressed each component of the definition of disability separately. Firstly, with reference to the EEOC regulations,[110] the Court accepted that a condition affecting the reproductive system was included within the definition of physical impairment.[111] Secondly, the Court reasoned that if it was included within the parameters of physical impairment, it was equally included within the scope of major life activities.[112] In doing so, it relied on *McWright*,[113] in which the CoA held that physical impairments affecting the reproductive system were included within its scope.[114] This reasoning was criticised for automatically assuming that impairments are disabilities,[115] a point previously raised in the Canadian context and in *Zatarain v WDSU-Television, Inc.*,[116] discussed later. Thirdly, adopting a common-sense approach, the Court held that infertility must substantially limit the major life function of reproduction.[117] Consequently, it held that she was disabled under the ADA.

The Court separately addressed the issues of sex and pregnancy discrimination, discussed in Chapter 4. However, in considering the nature of infertility, it refused to accept that it was a gender-neutral condition and that the experiences of women and men were the same.[118] Instead, the Court focused on the interrelationship between infertility and pregnancy, including potential pregnancy.[119] While the Court did not directly or explicitly consider this in an intersectional way, instead addressing each ground separately, the decisions relating to each characteristic are

---

109 *Ibid*, 1404.
110 29 CFR, §1630.2(h)(1).
111 *Pacourek* (n.107), 1404.
112 *Ibid*, 1404–5.
113 Decided under the Rehabilitation Act of 1973, 29 USC §701 et seq. The relevant provisions being substantially similar to those in the ADA, with related decisions and reasoning equally applicable here: *Ibid*, 1405.
114 *McWright* (n.89), [19].
115 Timothy D Johnston, 'Reproduction Is Not a Major Life Activity: Implications for HIV Infection as a Per Se Disability under the Americans with Disabilities Act' [1999] 85 Cornell L Rev 189, 221–22.
116 881 F.Supp.240 (ED La 1995).
117 *Pacourek* (n.107), 1405.
118 *Ibid*, 1403–4.
119 *Ibid*, 1401.

inherently interrelated. By accepting that infertility has sex-specific consequences relating to childbearing capacity, this reinforces the unique experiences of women undergoing treatment. In addition, by acknowledging that
reproduction is a major life activity, the Court recognises not only the social
value of procreation but also the position of women, who are more likely
to experience barriers to engagement in society in relation to reproduction-
related impairments.

Dallmann notes that this decision shows how the ADA can be interpreted
broadly to include a range of 'non-traditional disabilities,' with the key consideration being the willingness of courts to accept reproduction as a major
life activity.[120] However, it was equally open to the courts to interpret it
more narrowly. This was the case in the District Court decision *Zatarain*, in
which the plaintiff claimed disability discrimination when her contract was
not renewed while she was undergoing ART treatments.[121] Her employer
was again aware of this as her schedule had already been changed to accommodate undergoing treatment.[122] However, during the contract negotia-
tions, she informed them that further changes were recommended, which
they were unwilling to accept, particularly as she would not agree to a wage
reduction, although she did offer to do additional work instead.

As in *Pacourek*, the Court addressed each element of the definition in
turn. Firstly, as in *Pacourek*, it accepted that Zatarain had a physical impairment. The employers had argued that the infertility was not related to a
physiological condition but was instead attributable to age- or work-related
stress. Despite being unexplained, the Court accepted the medical evidence
that it was distinct from these factors.[123] The decision is notable in this
respect, because the Court could have drawn distinctions between 'social
infertility' and/or unexplained infertility and infertility relating to a deter-
minable physiological condition. Nevertheless, it left open the possibility
for 'social' or unexplained infertility to be distinguished here.

Secondly, the Court considered whether reproduction was a major life
activity. In doing so, it criticised the reasoning in *Pacourek* as circular and
unpersuasive because the major life activity affected should be distinct from
the impairment itself. Johnston agreed that this was necessary to avoid
inferring that all elements of the definition are satisfied from the impairment alone.[124] However, Dallmann argued that this reasoning failed to

---

120 Dallmann (n.103), 398.
121 *Zatarain* (n.116), 242.
122 *Ibid*, 241–42.
123 *Ibid*, 242–43.
124 Johnston (n.115), 224.

apply the EEOC regulations accurately and identified that there were other instances where the impairment and major life activity were inseparable, for example visual or aural impairments which substantially limit the major life activities of seeing and hearing, respectively.[125] However, the Court held that including reproduction within the scope of major life activities was inconsistent with those noted in the illustrative guidance, which in the Court's view were all day-to-day activities. They reasoned that since one does not reproduce on a day-to-day basis, it could not be a major life activity. Dallmann argued that there was nothing in the guidance that required the activity be undertaken on such a frequent basis. Nonetheless, given that the reproductive system involves complex biological processes that the body goes through on a continual basis, all of which contribute to the possibility of conception, viewed holistically, it was a day-to-day activity.[126] Nevertheless, the Court concluded that the only possible activity engaged here was her ability to work.[127]

Thirdly, in considering whether infertility had a substantial impact on her ability to work, the Court referred to the EEOC regulations which stated that in order for an impairment to substantially impact on work, it related broadly to an inability to perform a particular class of jobs or a wide range of jobs across different classes. The inability to perform a particular job was not enough to satisfy this requirement.[128] Since Zatarain could still work as an anchor, albeit in a different working pattern to accommodate her treatment, this condition was not satisfied here.[129] Consequently, the Court held that she was not disabled under the ADA. In delivering her judgement, Judge Vance specifically noted that extending the definition to include infertility would amount to 'a conscious expansion of the law.'[130] However, Tomkowicz argued that the decision to hide behind the veil of judicial restraint was unjustified given the pre-existing authorities supporting such an interpretation.[131]

The decision in *Zatarain* adopted the same approach as that in the UK and the EU in defining disability. By focusing on whether the individual

---

125 Dallmann (n.103), 401–2.
126 *Ibid*, 403.
127 *Zatarain* (n.116), 243.
128 *Ibid*, 243–44.
129 *Ibid*, 244.
130 *Ibid*, 243.
131 Tomkowicz (n.48), 1069–78. Also: Dallmann (n.103), 404–11; Kristina M. Hall, 'Pacourek v Inland Steel Company: Enforcing Equal Protection Rights by Designating Infertility as a Disability Under the American's with Disabilities Act' [1997] 11(2) BYU J Pub L 287, 296–99.

is incapable of working, the Court focused solely on the functional ability of the individual to work rather than on the broader impact of the impairment, including on work. In *Zatarain*, the decision was constrained because reproduction was not included as a major life activity, hence why this issue did not arise in *Pacourek*. Nevertheless, the restrictive view on the impact on work reinforces the failure of the Court to consider this through the specific intersecting lenses of disability and gender, which was not raised here. Had such an approach been adopted, the gendered experience of undergoing ART treatments and its impact on workplace engagement would have been clearer and could have extended protection here.

However, the decision in *Zatarain* was subsequently followed in *Krauel v Iowa Methodist Medical Center*,[132] which was concerned with access to medical insurance coverage for ART treatments. In this case, both the District Court and the 8th Circuit CoA doubted the reasoning in *Pacourek* in relation to its interpretation of major life activity. Instead, they held that reproduction was a lifestyle choice and so was incapable of falling within the definition of disability under the ADA.[133] Tomkowicz argued that characterising reproduction as a lifestyle choice was problematic because it failed to acknowledge the lived experiences of those with fertility issues and the impact of those issues on their lives,[134] which is comparable with many other disabilities. It also reinforced similar arguments found in the context of pregnancy discrimination, explored further in Chapter 4. In addition, the Courts held that infertility was a gender-neutral condition,[135] again failing to acknowledge the unique experiences of women undergoing treatment. There are two notable characteristics of these decisions. Firstly, they fail to acknowledge the significance of procreation and so undervalue the role of childbearing and its implications for other activities, such as employment.[136] Secondly, they assume that infertility and its consequences are gender-neutral and in doing so fail to recognise that interrelationship between disability and gender in this context. This again reinforces the distinctions between these lines of cases, whereby disability is only recognised when viewed alongside acknowledgement of the gender-specific nature of infertility and its consequences for women.

While these cases indicated a shift away from recognising infertility as a disability, the decision in *Pacourek* was affirmed in *Erickson v Board of Governors of State Colleges*,[137] in which the plaintiff similarly claimed that

132 915 F.Supp.102 (SD Iowa 1995) (DC) affirmed 95 F.3d 674 (CoA).
133 *Krauel* (DC)(n.132), 107–8; (CoA)(n.132), 677.
134 Tomkowicz (n.48), 1076.
135 *Krauel* (DC)(n.132), 112–13; (CoA)(n.132), 680.
136 Dallmann (n.103), 401–4.
137 911 F.Supp.316 (ND Ill 1995).

she had been discriminated against on the grounds of her disability by her employer for legitimately using the sick leave policy to take time off to undergo ART treatments.[138] In doing so, the Illinoian District Court explicitly rejected the narrow interpretation adopted in *Zatarain*, particularly the focus on conception as a single act as opposed to recognising the ongoing complex biological process involved,[139] and affirmed the decision in *McWright*.[140] The employer in *Pacourek* subsequently sought summary judgement in relation to the ADA claim,[141] thus offering another opportunity for the Illinoian District Courts to review the competing authorities on this point. The Court followed the same line of reasoning as the earlier Court and determined that she satisfied all the requirements for disability. It dismissed the reasoning and decisions rejecting the original decision as oversimplifying and misunderstanding it.[142] In particular, it noted that *Zatarain* and *Krauel* defined major life activities far too narrowly and focused on the quantity rather than the quality of the activities. Such an approach was inconsistent with the EEOC regulations, which supported a broader definition. In addition, the Court reasoned that these cases trivialised reproduction, which was supported by the inclusion of work as a major life activity but not reproduction,[143] thus failing to recognise the gendered implications of that decision. This again reinforced the significance of interpreting disability through the intersecting lens of gender. However, the decision in *Zatarain* was also affirmed on appeal to the 5th Circuit CoA.[144] These inconsistent judgements reinforced the need for greater clarity regarding whether infertility is a disability.[145]

Infertility as disability: reproduction confirmed as 'a major life activity'

The question of whether reproduction is a major life activity was finally settled in the Supreme Court decision, *Bragdon v Abbott*,[146] although the

---

138 *Ibid*, 320–23.
139 *Ibid*, 322.
140 *Ibid*.
141 *Pacourek v Inland Steel Company* 916 F.Supp.797 (ND Ill 1996).
142 *Ibid*, 800–4.
143 *Ibid*, 804.
144 *Zatarain v WDSU-Television, Inc.* 79 F.3d 1143 (5th Cir 1996).
145 Dallmann (n.103), 401. Although such inconsistency is not limited to infertility: Catherine J. Lanctot, 'Ad Hoc Decision Making and Per Se Prejudice: How Individualizing the Determination of Disability Undermines the ADA' [1997] 42(2) Vill L Rev 327.
146 524 US 624 (1998).

decision and reasoning themselves are not without criticism.[147] The case was concerned with whether asymptomatic HIV was a disability rather than the question of whether infertility was within the scope of the ADA, although it was also viewed as a victory for infertile women.[148] The Court reasoned that reproduction was a major life activity since it is central to the life process,[149] again reinforcing the societal value of procreation. It rejected the argument that the life activity had to have a public or economic element with reference to guidance on similar terms in the Rehabilitation Act 1973, which included personal care and performing manual tasks, neither of which they considered were inherently public or economic activities.[150] Furthermore, the Court concluded that the impairment substantially limited this major life activity because an HIV-infected woman could not attempt to conceive without putting her partner and child at risk of contracting the infection. Therefore, substantially limiting her ability to engage in this major life activity.[151] The reasoning of the Court is notable because they reinforced that the major life activity must only be substantially limited and not impossible for the person to engage in.[152] This is equally significant in the context of infertility since a person may be considered disabled per the ADA yet be using ART treatments to be able to have a child. This issue was addressed in *Saks v Franklin Covey*,[153] discussed later. The Supreme Court decision reinforces that it is not what a person can or cannot do that is important but whether it is substantially more difficult for them to do so as a consequence of their impairment than it is for someone who does not have an impairment that is the appropriate consideration.

Its application to infertility was confirmed in the District Court decision, *Saks*, which was concerned with whether the exclusion of ART treatments from the employers' insurance coverage violated the ADA. While the Court held that her physical impairment of infertility substantially limited her ability to reproduce, which was a major life activity per *Bragdon*,[154] it noted that infertility caused by the normal ageing process was excluded.[155]

147 Johnston (n.115), 225–68.
148 Sherena Shawrieh, 'Bragdon v Abbott: Expanding the Reach of the Americans with Disabilities Act' [2000] 67(1) Defense Counsel Journal 106; Peter K. Rydel, 'Redefining the Right to Reproduce: Asserting Infertility as a Disability under the Americans with Disabilities Act' [1999] 63 Alb L Rev 593, 630–35.
149 *Bragdon* (n.146), 638.
150 *Ibid*, 638–39.
151 *Ibid*, 639–42.
152 *Ibid*, 641.
153 117 F.Supp.2d 318, 325–26.
154 *Ibid*, 324–25.
155 *Ibid*, 326.

This revisited the issue raised in *Zatarain*. Nevertheless, the Court held that the exclusion of insurance coverage was not contrary to the ADA because the insurance plan did not offer greater coverage to fertile people than to infertile people.[156] They adopted similar reasoning when considering the sex discrimination claim, which they easily dismissed since the policy applied equally to women and men.[157] The presumption that the plan was not discriminatory because it applied equally to both groups was inherently problematic, because it failed to recognise that an asymmetrical approach may be more appropriate to achieve equality. In this instance, the absence of support for fertility treatments does not disadvantage fertile employees because they have no reason to have recourse to them.[158] Consequently, the differences in the experiences of accessing insurance coverage are based solely on infertility, which the Court accepted as a disability under the ADA. Sato argues that the Court failed to conduct a disparate impact analysis here to determine whether this seemingly neutral policy did have an impact on disabled persons.[159] Had they done so, Sato argues it would have been clear that it was discriminatory towards infertile employees.[160] In particular, the case highlights the continuing challenges for those involved in ART treatments and this idea that they are only 'a little bit disabled.'[161] As Sato examines, a particular difficulty in this case was that it was raised under Title I ADA, which only requires equal treatment and does not require employers to take additional steps to ensure substantive equality in the application of insurance coverage.[162] Furthermore, by failing to recognise the gendered experience of undergoing treatment and its inherent connection with childbearing, the Court again failed to extend protection. By adopting a symmetrical approach in its analysis of the extent of coverage and directly comparing coverage of infertility between women and men,[163] the Court failed to acknowledge the greater burdens on women that an intersectionality approach would have recognised. This again demonstrates that protection is only extended when these intersections are acknowledged.

---

156 *Ibid*, 326–28.
157 *Ibid*, 328.
158 Shorge Sato, 'A Little Bit Disabled: Infertility and the Americans with Disabilities Act' [2001] 5 NYUJ Legis & Pub Pol'y 189, 216.
159 *Ibid*, 215–18.
160 *Ibid*, 218.
161 *Ibid*, 191.
162 *Ibid*, 208–14.
163 *Saks* (n.153), 328.

This was subsequently considered in the District Court decision *LaPorta v Wal-Mart Stores, Inc.*,[164] which was concerned with dismissal related to undergoing ART treatment. LaPorta was already working a reduced schedule following an accident when she began ART treatments.[165] She advised her employer that she would require additional time off to undergo IVF treatment, and it was agreed that she would use annual leave for such purposes and that it would support her.[166] However, during her second cycle of treatment, she requested one day off work to undergo time-sensitive treatment, which her employer refused because it claimed it was unable to cover it. She was subsequently dismissed both for failing to attend and because she could not work her original hours, which had been reduced following her accident and had not previously been raised as a concern. The Court again upheld that infertility was a disability, following the reasoning in *Bragdon* and *Saks* in particular.[167] In doing so, it rejected the approach adopted in the so-called *Sutton* trilogy of cases,[168] which held that corrective measures or treatments should be taken into account when determining if someone is disabled, particularly in relation to whether the impairment substantially limits a major life activity.[169] Abney argues that this strategy was the only way in which the Courts could reason that infertility was not a disability, since it had been accepted that it satisfied all the criteria in the definition.[170] Nevertheless, the Court held that ART treatments did not cure infertility but rather assisted women in achieving that normal bodily function. The fact that some women, including LaPorta, were ultimately successful in achieving pregnancy did not prevent infertility from being considered a disability. The Court also considered that the accommodation sought here, the one-day absence, was *prima facie* a reasonable one.[171] The reasoning adopted by the Court here again recognises the inherently gendered nature of treatment and its implications for women's workplace engagement, although it is notable that the Court did not consider infertility to be a pregnancy-related condition.[172] Nevertheless, any remaining uncertainty

164   163 F.Supp.2d 758 (WD Mich 2001).
165   *Ibid*, 761.
166   *Ibid*, 762.
167   *LaPorta* (n.164), 764–66.
168   *Sutton v United Air Lines* 119 S Ct 2139 (1999); *Murphy v United Parcel Service* 119 S Ct 2133 (1999); and *Albertsons Inc. v Kirkingburg*, 119 S Ct 2162 (1999).
169   *LaPorta* (n.164), 765–66.
170   Teresa M Abney, 'Working Women Seeking Infertility Treatments: Does the ADA or Title VII Offer Any Protection?' [2009] 58(1) Drake L Rev 295, 305–8.
171   *LaPorta* (n.164), 766–68.
172   *Ibid*, 770–71, discussed in Chapter 4.

surrounding the question of whether infertility is a disability has arguably been placed beyond doubt following the 2008 ADA amendments.[173] These explicitly included reproduction as 'a major life activity', thus endorsing the approach adopted in the jurisprudence determining that infertility was a disability. This was also reinforced in the amendment specifically overruling the *Sutton* trilogy cases.[174] Abney argues that it now seems clear that infertility is a disability under the ADA, although questions may remain regarding its underlying cause,[175] as suggested in *Saks*, indicating that it may not include everyone undergoing ART treatment.

The development of the scope of disability in the US suggests that an intersectionality approach is necessary to expand the boundaries of protection in this context. While the Courts did not explicitly adopt an intersectionality approach, it is clear that the interrelationship between gender and disability was key in those decisions accepting infertility as a disability. These decisions reinforce that acknowledging these interconnections is fundamental to recognising not only the social value of procreation but also the significant impact that childbearing has on women's working lives, irrespective of the stage in the process under consideration. This experience indicates that adopting a broad interpretation of disability that is influenced by the social model and acknowledges the inherently gendered experience of undergoing ART treatments is necessary to include infertility within the scope of disability. This final section now turns to examine whether, drawing from this experience, the interpretation of disability in the UK can be re-interpreted to also include infertility.

Reinterpreting disability: lessons for the UK

McCarn noted that adopting a medical model definition of disability would mean that 'it would be static and unresponsive to social change.'[176] This is borne out by the way in which disability has been interpreted in the UK and how the legislation has not been amended following the UK ratification of the CRPD.[177] This raises the question of whether it is capable of being

173 ADA Amendments Act of 2008. Pub L No.110–325 122 Stat 3553; Abney (n.169), 306–8.

174 ADA, §12102(4)(E); discussed *Ibid*, 308.

175 *Ibid*, 308–9.

176 Alison A McCarn, 'Rights Not Charity: An Analysis of the Models of Disability and Their Contribution to the Construction and Interpretation of the Definition of Disability under the Disability Discrimination Act 1995' [2003] 6(2) CIL 103, 116.

177 Lawson (n.76), 362–63; Sarah Fraser Butlin, 'The UN Convention on the Rights of Persons with Disabilities: Does the Equality Act 2010 Measure Up to UK International Commitments?' [2011] 40(4) ILJ 428.

interpreted more broadly to include infertility within its boundaries. However, the ratification of the CRPD, including its recognition of multiple discrimination, provides the opportunity to do so in the way envisioned by the intersectional analysis adopted here. The US experience also demonstrates that even when an intersectional analysis is not explicitly referred to, considering infertility through the lenses of both disability and gender have resulted in infertility being accepted as a disability. The connection between the ADA and the UK framework is also notable, since comparisons were drawn with this in the development of the Disability Discrimination Act 1995 (DDA).[178] Drawing from this, this final section argues that a broader interpretation is possible in the UK, which could include infertility as a disability.

An alternative interpretation of disability

While not directly applicable, the CRPD requires state parties to ensure the human rights and fundamental freedoms of persons with disabilities are realised and that they are protected against all kinds of discrimination.[179] It is included within the definition of Community Conventions under s.1(2) of the European Communities Act 1972, which means its provisions must be given effect to in UK law per s.2(1). Section 4 of the European Union Withdrawal Act 2018 ensures that these rights and legal obligations become part of domestic law post-Brexit. Furthermore, as an independent signatory, the UK remains required to ensure that it is implemented into domestic law. The CRPD should thus be considered when interpreting and applying domestic law, including the application of the EqA. This means that it is possible for the courts to draw from the Convention when interpreting the boundaries of disability and, in doing so, adopt a definition that is more reflective of the social model underpinning the CRPD[180] and capable of including infertility as a disability.

The CRPD also recognises multiple discrimination, particularly from the perspective of disabled women and girls in Art.6(1). State parties are required to take appropriate action to address this and empower disabled women so that they can exercise the rights included in the Convention.[181] Multiple discrimination is also referred to in preamble paras. 17 and 19, with 19 endorsing the importance of adopting 'a gender perspective in all efforts to promote

178 Brian Doyle, 'Employment Rights, Equal Opportunities and Disabled Persons: The Ingredients for Reform' [1993] 22(2) IJL 89, 90; McCarn (n.176), 113.
179 Art.4.
180 Butlin (n.177), 428.
181 Art.6(2). Fredman (n.76), 36.

the full enjoyment of human rights and fundamental freedoms by persons with disabilities.' Furthermore, intersectional discrimination is one of the areas that the Committee on the Rights of Persons with Disabilities recommended the UK address.[182] Adopting an intersectionality analysis using the intersecting lenses of disability and gender would be consistent with this.

Before focusing on disability, it is useful to note that a primarily symmetrical approach is adopted in relation to sex discrimination under s.11 EqA. As noted earlier, the experiences of infertility for women and men do not afford meaningful comparisons, unlike those between infertile women and those who conceive naturally.[183] However, the current framework specifically excludes this kind of comparison in s.11(b) since they share this protected characteristic. Nevertheless, those undergoing treatment are primarily infertile women, because it is inherently connected with childbearing capacity, which is biologically sex-specific. In this context, an asymmetrical approach is required. This mirrors the disability framework and reinforces that examining infertility through these intersecting lenses is necessary to acknowledge the gendered implications of infertility and reinterpret the definition of disability.

Disability is defined in s.6(1) and contains four components: physical or mental impairment; which has a substantial; long-term adverse effect; on the ability to carry out normal day-to-day activities. Further guidance is provided in Sch.1. The legislation adopts a functional medical model of disability, although s.13 allows claims based on perceptions of disability, and associative discrimination is included following (C-303/06) *Coleman v Attridge Law (A Firm)*,[184] recognising some of the societal barriers and mirroring the US approach. Each of the components is examined through the intersecting lenses of disability and gender and the US experience to determine whether infertility can be interpreted as satisfying each component of disability.

Firstly, the individual must show that he or she has a physical or mental impairment, with infertility likely to be a physical impairment. The UK jurisprudence indicates that the term *impairment* is to be given its ordinary meaning,[185] and there is no need to establish an underpinning medical

182 Committee on the Rights of Persons with Disabilities, *Concluding Observations on the Initial Report of the United Kingdom of Great Britain and Northern Ireland* (CRPD/C/GBR/CO/1, 2017), [15], [19].
183 As mentioned by AG Kokott in *CD* (n.1), although considered out with the scope of ETD.
184 [2008] ECR I-5603.
185 *McNicol v Balfour Beatty Rail Maintenance Ltd* [2002] ICR 1498, Mummery LJ, [17]; Office for Disability Matters, *Equality Act 2010 Guidance: Guidance on Matters to be Taken into Account in Determining Questions Relating to the Definition of Disability* (HM Government 2011) A3.

condition or illness.[186] This may be particularly useful for infertility as the underlying reason is not always known and/or cannot be explained. Such an interpretation would be consistent with the US jurisprudence, which largely accepted that infertility is a physical impairment, although this was limited in *Saks* where infertility relating to social factors such as age were considered outside its scope. While the question of whether infertility is a disability has not been directly considered in the UK, the decision in *Murphy* suggests that similar constraints would have been applied by the UK courts.

In *Murphy*, the Courts all accepted that she was disabled per the DDA in relation to her congenital heart condition.[187] In reaching its decision, the ET appeared to draw distinctions between this and infertility itself, suggesting that those with specific fertility issues, such as 'fallopian tube problems,' would not have been covered.[188] While the EAT concluded that Murphy had been treated less favourably for a reason related to her disability, namely her inability to have children,[189] it is unclear whether it meant that the inability itself was the disability or whether it was a consequence of her underlying condition. However, given the comments of the ET and the acceptance that the heart condition was a disability, the latter interpretation is most likely. Nevertheless, given the advances, not only in medicine but also in legal thinking, particularly drawing from the US experience, it would be reasonable for UK courts to now accept that infertility is a physical impairment and so satisfies this requirement.

Secondly, the individual must show that it has an impact on their ability to perform normal day-to-day activities. There is potential for broadening the scope of protection here since normal day-to-day activities are no longer defined in the legislation.[190] The government issued non-exhaustive guidance, which provides illustrative examples of what is included here,[191] but it does not expressly consider fertility-related issues. It does state that day-to-day activities include things people generally do on a daily or regular basis.[192] It further notes that they need not be undertaken by the majority of people, and some may only be carried out by members of one sex,[193]

---

186 *Millar v Inland Revenue Commissioners* [2005] CSIH 71, 2006 SC 155, [23]; Office for Disability Matters (n.185), A3.
187 *Murphy* (EAT) (n.1), [39]; (CoA)(n.1), [6].
188 *Ibid* (EAT), [32] referring to [14] of the ET decision.
189 *Ibid*, [39].
190 Previously: DDA, Sch.1, para.4(1).
191 Office for Disability Matters, (n.185), D2–D24.
192 *Ibid*, D3.
193 *Ibid*, D5.

thus recognising that some activities are sex-specific and indicating that a gendered analysis is necessary for determining if they are day-to-day activities.

While reproduction in the sense of trying to conceive and/or being pregnant is not necessarily a daily activity, it is something that most people will engage in during their lives. Furthermore, for those with actual or potential fertility issues, reproduction becomes an inherent aspect of their day-to-day lives and activities. Moreover, as the US jurisprudence shows, the reproductive system involves many continuous complex processes that have an impact on fertility. Viewed in these terms, an impairment of the reproductive system is an impairment that impacts on day-to-day activities.[194] Consequently, analysing day-to-day activities through the intersecting lenses of disability and gender enables the interrelated experiences of infertility and reproduction to be acknowledged. Adopting this understanding also broadens the scope of protection to better include conditions affecting women, which are often invisible and more difficult to reconcile with traditional perceptions of disability. Furthermore, this would be consistent with the CRPD requirement to take account of multidimensional discrimination, particularly from the perspective of women. Thus, viewing disability from a gendered perspective would reinforce that reproduction is a normal day-to-day activity.

This would also be consistent with Art.23(1) CRPD which requires state parties to eliminate discrimination in relation to parenthood and relationships, to ensure that disabled people have the same rights to found a family and freely choose the number and spacing of children as persons without disabilities. This includes ensuring that the mechanisms are in place to enable them to exercise these rights. This is not concerned with defining day-to-day activities but instead reflects the inherent value of procreation and the historical challenges disabled people faced in gaining control over reproductive choice and childbearing capacity. Nevertheless, recognising reproduction as a normal day-to-day activity acknowledges this, particularly from the perspective of disabled women, and underscores the value of childbearing and reproductive choice.

Thirdly, the impairment must have a substantial impact on their ability to carry out normal day-to-day activities. In *Goodwin v The Patent Office*, this was interpreted by Morison J as meaning 'more than minor or trivial' rather than 'very large.'[195] The guidance identifies various factors that can be taken into account in determining if the impact is substantial, including

---

194 As in *Erikson* (n.137), 322.
195 [1999] ICR 302, 310.

the time taken to carry out an activity, the way in which an activity is carried out; cumulative effects of an impairment, effect on behaviour and effects of the environment.[196] Being infertile would have a substantial impact on carrying out the normal day-to-day activity of reproduction, particularly the time taken or the way in which the activity is carried out. However, this is dependent on reproduction being considered a normal day-to-day activity in the first instance. This would again mirror the approach adopted in the US jurisprudence which accepts that infertility substantially limits the major life activity of reproduction, since it is more difficult for infertile women to become pregnant than those without fertility issues. A similar approach could be adopted in the UK since it equally does not require that it be impossible to undertake the activity, only that it is more difficult to do so because of the impairment. Consequently, analysing the experience of infertility through the intersecting lenses of disability and gender again justifies interpreting infertility as having a substantial impact on normal day-to-day activities.

The final condition is that the impairment must have a long-term adverse effect, defined in Sch.1, para.2 as the effect having lasted, or likely to last, for at least 12 months or for the rest of their life. Those with fertility issues should also be able to satisfy this condition, particularly since one of the factors required to diagnose infertility is the inability to conceive after one year of actively trying.[197] This would mean that there would be sufficient continuing adverse effects from the impairment (the cause of infertility) on a day-to-day activity (reproduction) for the requisite period. Consequently, the current UK definition of disability offers the potential for infertility to fall within its scope. This is primarily dependent on adopting a broad interpretation of normal day-to-day activities in the first instance and recognising the gendered experiences of infertility in interpreting the requirements of the definition. Nevertheless, the US experience reinforces that such reinterpretations are possible, particularly when viewed through the intersecting lenses of disability and gender.

Accepting that infertility is a disability would enable those treated less favourably and/or dismissed for reasons relating to undergoing ART treatments to claim either direct discrimination (s.13), indirect discrimination (s.19) or discrimination arising in consequence of disability (s.15). Disability-related discrimination, the precursor to s.15, was indeed considered in *Murphy*. While the majority in the ET focused on the fact that she had chosen surrogacy, which it held was the reason for the difference in treatment, not her underlying disability;[198] the minority recognised that there was a direct link between the refusal of paid leave and her disability, because that was the reason she used a surrogate.[199] The EAT reinforced that 'the reason' in s.5(1) DDA refers to the reason for the less favourable treatment and does not include a requirement of a causal link with the disability.[200] Consequently, the EAT held that the reason for the less favourable treatment, in comparison with gestational mothers, was her inability to bear her own child. Thus, the decision not to afford her paid childcare leave was for a reason related to her disability.[201] This recognises the inherent interconnection between infertility and its gendered consequences, which are not limited to those undergoing treatment but are also exposed by gendered, and gestational, assumptions regarding appropriate childcare roles. A point that the CJEU failed to appreciate in *Z*. While s.15 now refers to 'unfavourable treatment because of something arising in consequence of disability,' a similar interpretation would be possible here. Using a surrogate was a consequence of her disability, and that was the reason for the unfavourable treatment. This indicates that the analysis of the interconnection between disability and infertility, including its consequences for workplace engagement, as suggested by scholars in the EU context,[202] would be accepted in the UK, further strengthening the potential of UK law to include infertility within the scope of protection.

Infertility and additional CRPD obligations

The CRPD contains other provisions which are also potentially relevant to those undergoing ART treatments. These include the promotion of equality for persons with disabilities in relation to equal treatment, equal protection and equal benefit from law.[203] State parties are also required to prohibit all forms of disability discrimination and guarantee effective legal protection against all forms of discrimination.[204] In addition to ensuring that rights are protected under equality law, this could include ensuring that relevant employment rights extend throughout the ART treatment period, enabling those undergoing treatment to combine this with employment.

---

198 *Murphy* (EAT) (n.1), [32] referring to [14] of the ET decision.
199 *Ibid*, [33].
200 *Murphy* (EAT) (n.1), [36]–[39].
201 *Ibid*, [39].
202 n.85.
203 Art.5(1).
204 Art.5(2).

A specific right to time off to undergo treatment is explored in Chapter 5 and could satisfy these obligations.

Furthermore, the Convention permits positive action[205] and requires that reasonable adjustments be made to both promote equality and eradicate discrimination.[206] This is further expanded in the context of protection against discrimination with respect to work and employment in Art.27, which includes making reasonable accommodations,[207] as defined in Art.2. For those undergoing ART treatments, this requirement could refer to changes to work schedules and/or the right to time off work to undergo treatments. An individual right to reasonable adjustments in employment is recognised in s.20 EqA and could include making changes to absence management policies allowing time off for treatment to prevent disadvantage arising from a provision, criterion or practice of the employer. This would be consistent with the US remedy of reasonable accommodation, which includes adjustments to work schedules, and is considered significant in this context because of the consequences of failing to accommodate infertility. For instance, Hall argues that those undergoing ART treatments must be protected to ensure that their fundamental constitutional rights to become parents are also protected.[208] This is supported by Dallmann, who argues that a lack of employment-related rights and protections may prevent women from utilising ART treatments because of its impact on work. Consequently, affording protection here is necessary to support a woman's childbearing rights.[209] Tomkowicz further argues that the right to reasonable accommodation can address the experiences of infertile women and meet the objectives of the ADA by removing the barriers that would otherwise prevent them from benefiting from the same workplace opportunities as persons without disabilities.[210] This focus on removing the barriers is consistent with the social model of disability and the recognition of the gendered experience of infertility, also reflecting Schiek's intersecting nodes approach. However, while s.20 facilitates this on an individualised basis, the lack of an overarching legal framework means that more can be done to remove societal barriers. Specific rights, as discussed in Chapter 5, could offer a meaningful way of both removing such barriers and promoting equality.

---

205 Art.5(4).
206 Art.5(3).
207 Art.27(1)(f).
208 Hall (n.131), 299.
209 Dallmann (n.103), 413.
210 Tomkowicz (n.48), 1089.

Conclusion

This chapter demonstrates that the definitions of disability in both the EU and the UK have been drawn too narrowly, thus excluding infertility and those engaged in ART treatments from their scope. However, it has also demonstrated that the current legislative frameworks can be interpreted more broadly by shifting the interpretative framework from an analysis of single axes of discrimination to acknowledge intersectional lived experiences. For those engaged in ART treatments, this involves examining the legislation through the intersecting lenses of disability and gender and, in doing so, recognising and embracing the social model of disability and the inherently gendered experiences of certain kinds of impairments. The US jurisprudence demonstrates the interconnection between disability and gender in this context, even without adopting an explicit intersectional analysis. Thus, recognising the significance of these intersections and the need for legal frameworks to extend protection here.

While there is no legal requirement for the UK to implement the US jurisprudence and amendments to the ADA, the UK has drawn from this before. This suggests that the underpinning purposes and frameworks of the legislation in both countries are similar and thus open to the possibility of consistent future development. Furthermore, the UK has committed itself to the CRPD, which itself drew from the US experience, including using it as an interpretative tool when applying UK law. Consequently, the parameters of UK legislation can be interpreted more broadly with reference to these frameworks, using the intersecting lenses of disability and gender as analytical tools. The application of these here suggests that this would facilitate a broadening of the scope of disability to include infertility. At a time when the UK is reflecting on the legal framework relating to surrogacy, this provides an appropriate opportunity to also reflect on how it relates to other areas of law and adopt a more coherent and strategic approach to recognising and protecting the position of all those engaged in ART treatments.

However, the limitations of the disability approach have also been apparent. In particular, there is the perception that infertility is not like other kinds of disabilities, which have more significant implications on the person's overall health.[211] This has led to infertile women being referred to as ' "a little bit disabled" and thus only a "little bit entitled" to their legal rights. . . '[212] This reinforces the underlying concern that while infertility

---

211 Sato (n.158), 200–2.
212 *Ibid*, 191.

might fall within the definition of disability, there is at least a perception that it does not deserve the same degree of protection as other disabilities do. Furthermore, a disability-focused approach inherently excludes certain groups who are utilising ART treatments for other reasons. For instance, it would exclude female same-sex partners and single women who choose to undergo ART treatments because they would otherwise be unable to conceive on their own. It would also exclude male same-sex partners and women who for personal, as opposed to medical, reasons choose to use surrogates in order to have a child that is biologically linked to at least one parent. This could also include instances where the cause of the infertility is unknown, and so not attributable to a specific physical impairment, or where it relates to a natural age-related decline in optimal fertility.[213] Consequently, while a disability-focused approach may include those most vulnerable to less favourable treatment and/or dismissal, it does not adequately encompass all those undergoing ART treatments. Consequently, examining the experiences of those engaged in ART treatments through an alternative analytical frame may offer a more inclusive approach.

213 Sato (n.158), 204; Abney (n.170), 308–9; *Saks* (n.153), 326.

4 Conceiving a new interpretation of pregnancy and sex discrimination
Redefining the boundaries

Introduction

In this chapter, the experiences of those undergoing ART treatments are examined through the primary lens of gender intersecting with disability, insofar as there is a requirement to accommodate difference. In doing so, it continues to draw from Schiek's intersecting nodes, this time focusing on sex and pregnancy, which Schiek identifies as being on the orbits of both gender and disability.[1] The chapter first examines two facets of discrimination addressed within the gender node, namely symmetrical treatment, ensuring that women (and men) are not treated differently because of stereotypical views on appropriate gender roles,[2] and asymmetrical treatment, recognising those instances were differential treatment is required to ensure equality for women, for instance recognising the impact of childbearing on workplace engagement.[3] Since pregnancy discrimination embraces the intersections between gender and disability, the underpinning rationale of protection is examined and compared with the experiences of those undergoing ART treatments. Despite the similarities, the pregnancy approach has failed to afford protection to those undergoing ART treatments because of the requirement for a pre-existing pregnancy. Revisiting the boundaries of sex discrimination, as attempted in Case C-506/06 *Mayr v Bäckerei und Konditorei*

---

1 Dagmar Schiek, 'Intersectionality and the Notion of Disability in EU Discrimination Law' [2016] 53 CML Rev 35, 52; Dagmar Schiek, 'On Uses, Mis-uses and Non-uses of Intersectionality before the Court of Justice (EU)' [2018] 18(2–3) IJDL 82, 88.
2 Dagmar Schiek, 'Organizing EU Equality Law Around the Nodes of "Race", Gender and Disability' in Dagmar Schiek and Anna Lawson (eds), *European Union Non-Discrimination Law and Intersectionality: Investigating the Triangle of Racial, Gender and Disability Discrimination* (Ashgate Publishing 2011) 24.
3 *Ibid.*

Gerhard Flöckner OHG,[4] offers the greatest potential to extend protection to all those undergoing ART treatments. Comparisons are drawn with the US jurisprudence, where protection against pregnancy-related discrimination in the Pregnancy Discrimination Act 1978 (PDA) has been extended to include those undergoing ART treatments.[5] The US experience again appears to implicitly adopt the kind of intersectional analysis envisaged here, focusing on the interconnection between childbearing capacity and the need to accommodate this, indicating that an alternative interpretation is possible. This is then applied to the UK context to determine whether the definition of pregnancy discrimination can be interpreted more broadly to include those undergoing ART treatments. Alternatively, a reinterpretation of sex discrimination is examined with reference to two low-level Scottish decisions,[6] which consider whether associative discrimination can be extended to those discriminated against on the grounds of someone else's pregnancy. This suggests that the boundaries of sex discrimination could be expanded further to fully protect those engaged in ART treatments throughout the treatment process.

Intersectionality and the boundaries of gender discrimination

Schiek's gender node encompasses both those instances when stereotypical gender norms must be challenged and women and men treated in the same way; as well as those when an asymmetrical approach is required, such as to accommodate pregnancy.[7] This underscores the inherent tensions between assuming that women are primary caregivers and/or may become pregnant, which undermines gender equality, while also recognising and valuing that women, at times, require accommodations based on childbearing capacity to achieve gender equality.[8] The important differences between these are that the former is based purely on ascriptions regarding appropriate gender roles whereas the latter reflects the lived experiences of women engaged in childbearing. These competing views on equality have posed conceptual and practical difficulties in applying symmetrical equal

---

4 [2008] 2 CMLR 27.
5 Pub L No.95–555, 92 Stat 2076 (codified at 42 USC §2000e(k)). *Pacourek v Inland Steel Co* 858 F.Supp.1393 (ND Ill 1994); *Erickson v Board of Governors of State Colleges and Universities for Northeastern Illinois Universities* 911 F.Supp.316 (ND Ill 1995); and *Hall v Nalco Co.* 534 F.3d 644 (7th Cir 2008).
6 *Kulikaoskas v Macduff Shellfish* [2011] ICR 48; *Gyenes v Highland Welcome (UK) Ltd t/a The Star Hotel* 2014 WL 10246834.
7 Schiek (n.2), 24.
8 *Ibid.*

treatment principles to asymmetrical experiences. This was evident in the development of pregnancy discrimination as an intersectional strand of sex discrimination, intersecting with disability, and is equally evident in the experiences of those undergoing ART treatments.

Pregnancy discrimination: from gender equality to specific rights

Given that pregnancy is now a separate protected characteristic in both the EU and the UK,[9] it is perhaps difficult to consider it as a form of intersectional discrimination. However, its emergence as a separate characteristic is rooted in such analyses of sex discrimination in the first instance. As Fredman argues, while pregnancy could be a subcategory of sex discrimination, it is only by adopting a capacious interpretation of sex that it falls within its scope.[10] This is because not all women are, can or will be pregnant, so it does not easily fall within the symmetrical sex discrimination paradigm. This is equally true for women engaged in ART treatments, who similarly represent a small subset of all women. Fredman argues that it is only by the courts recognising the 'specific intersecting axes of power that made a pregnant woman particularly disadvantaged in the paid workforce' that protection was extended.[11] This reflects the separate spheres ideology, which distinguishes between the private sphere of family, including women's reproductive capacity as well as caring responsibilities, and the public sphere of state, market and work.[12] The feminist construction of the separate spheres ideology reinforces the invisibility of family and caring

---

9 Directive 2006/54/EC of the European Parliament and of the Council of 5 July 2006 on the implementation of the principle of equal opportunities and equal treatment of men and women in matters of employment and occupation (recast), Art.2(2)(c) (ETD), with reference to Council Directive 92/85/EEC of 19 October 1992 on the introduction of measures to encourage improvements in the safety and health at work of pregnant workers and workers who have recently given birth or are breastfeeding, Art.2 (PWD); s.18 Equality Act 2010 (EqA).

10 Sandra Fredman, 'Intersectional Discrimination in EU Gender Equality and Non-discrimination Law' (European Network of Legal Experts in Gender Equality and Non-discrimination, European Commission 2016) 11, 73.

11 *Ibid*, 73.

12 Frances E Olsen, 'The Family and the Market: A Study of Ideology and Legal Reform' [1983] 96(7) Harvard L Rev 1497, 1497–530; M.D.A. Freeman, 'Towards a Critical Theory of Family Law' [1985] 38(1) CLP 153, 166–68; Margaret Thornton, 'The Public/Private Dichotomy: Gendered and Discriminatory' [1991] 18(4) JL Soc'y 448, 449–51; Sandra Fredman, *Women and the Law* (OUP 1997) 16–17.

responsibilities within the private sphere from the public sphere of work.[13] Such invisibility makes it difficult for women to both claim equal treatment while also ensuring that differences are accommodated. This reasoning is equally applicable to the experiences of those undergoing ART treatments, with women being disadvantaged by the same intersecting axes of power, particularly around the unburdened male worker norm.[14] This was particularly evident in the development of pregnancy discrimination within the boundaries of the symmetrical sex discrimination paradigm.

Following the CJEU decision in (C-177/88) *Dekker v Stichting Vormingscentrum voor Jonge Volwassenen Plus*,[15] pregnancy discrimination was recognised as inherently direct sex discrimination because pregnancy could not be separated from gender.[16] This presented a shift from symmetrical to asymmetrical treatment and suggested that a comparator was no longer necessary since pregnancy discrimination was recognised as direct sex discrimination. However, this interpretation of the decision was criticised. Instead, it was argued that a comparator was still required and that indirect sex discrimination was more appropriate.[17] Such an approach was problematic because it treated pregnancy, at best, as if it were an illness[18] and, at worst, as a lifestyle choice, like growing a beard,[19] that only some women choose. However, the conceptual and practical challenges in accepting pregnancy discrimination as a form of direct sex discrimination can be located in the requirement to accommodate difference.[20] Conceptualising this through the intersecting lenses of gender and disability addresses this concern because it recognises that the accommodation of difference is justified not just because pregnancy is sex-specific but also because it is inherently related to childbearing capacity. Accommodating this is fundamental to ensuring gender equality in the workplace.

13 Olsen (n.12), 1504–7; Freeman (n.12), 168–74; Katherine O'Donovan, *Sexual Divisions in Law* (Weidenfeld and Nicolson 1985) 11–12, 14–15; Gillian More, 'Equal Treatment in European Community Law: The Limits of Market Equality' in Anne Bottomley (ed), *Feminist Perspectives on the Foundational Subjects of Law* (Cavendish Publishing Limited 1996) 261–65; Fredman (n.12), 183–92.

14 Grace James, *The Legal Regulation of Pregnancy and Parenting* (Routledge-Cavendish 2009) 17–18.

15 [1992] ICR 325.

16 *Ibid*, [12]; Sandra Fredman, 'A Difference with Distinction: Pregnancy and Parenthood Reassessed' [1994] 110(January) LQR 106, 114.

17 Robert Wintemute, 'When is Pregnancy Discrimination Indirect Sex Discrimination?' [1998] 27(1) ILJ 23.

18 *Ibid*, 28–35.

19 *Ibid*, 27.

20 Simon Honeyball, 'Pregnancy and Sex Discrimination' [2000] 29(1) ILJ 43.

This is analogous with the position of those undergoing ART treatments and reinforces similar challenges with comparing ART treatments with illness. While both women and men can be infertile, those most vulnerable to less favourable treatment are women undergoing treatment, which is related to their childbearing capacity, irrespective of the reasons for utilising treatment. Comparisons with men are unhelpful because they are not in comparable positions while undergoing treatment. The important consideration here is the inherent interconnection between undergoing ART treatment and the potential for pregnancy that it offers. It is in this key respect that the experiences of infertility differ and why women should be afforded protection. To analyse infertility as gender-neutral is to adopt a male perspective, examining it through the sole lens of infertility as a medical condition wholly unrelated to pregnancy.[21] It is only by adopting a gendered analysis, focusing on childbearing capacity, that the unique experiences of women are acknowledged. Reverting to the ill-man comparator and/or the idea of reproduction being a lifestyle choice is inappropriate because it problematises reproduction rather than normalising alternative routes to parenthood. In the same way that accommodation of pregnancy required to be normalised by the legal framework, so, too, do the experiences of those undergoing ART treatments. Honeyball suggested that the appropriate comparison for pregnancy discrimination was to compare the position the pregnant woman was in with that she would have been in had she not been pregnant, thus isolating the discriminating factor.[22] He argued that such an approach removed the requirement for comparison with a male norm while retaining the need to draw comparisons. This is similar to AG Kokott's suggestion that comparing a commissioning mother with a woman who did not use surrogacy arrangements would be most appropriate, although outside the scope of the ETD.[23] This kind of conceptual approach and reasoning would also be useful in the context of all those engaged in ART treatments.

In this respect, it is useful to reflect on the US Supreme Court decision *California Savings and Loan Association v Guerra*.[24] Marshall J reasoned that women's rights to equal participation in the workplace could only be achieved by ensuring that they, like men, could have families without losing

21 As explored further in the discussion of US cases discussed later and in Cintra D. Bentley, 'A Pregnant Pause: Are Women Who Undergo Fertility Treatment to Achieve Pregnancy within the Scope of Title VII's Pregnancy Discrimination Act' [1998] 73 Chi-Kent L Rev 391, 415–19.
22 Honeyball (n.20), 49.
23 Case C-167/12 *CD v ST* [2014] 3 CMLR 15, [AG87].
24 479 US 272 (1987).

their jobs.[25] While Marshall J is referring to pregnancy-related benefits, this is equally true for those undergoing ART treatments as this is how they hope to have families, which they should equally be able to do without losing their jobs. Furthermore, as Fredman argued, the social value of procreation must be acknowledged so that women do not bear the burden of reproduction alone.[26] While she was also not specifically contemplating those undergoing ART treatments, the same rings true, irrespective of the route to parenthood. To hold otherwise would be to say that women undergoing ART treatments must bear that burden alone. Consequently, the arguments that have been raised in the context of sex and pregnancy discrimination must now be reframed to acknowledge the different routes to parenthood that now exist, particularly from the perspective of women undergoing ART treatments.

The limitations of pregnancy discrimination

While the comparison with pregnancy discrimination is conceptually consistent with the experiences of those undergoing ART treatments, its extension here is problematic because of the way in which pregnancy protections have developed. This is evident in the CJEU jurisprudence which has uneasily addressed the distinctions between equality and difference by reinforcing the protection of the 'special relationship between a mother and her child.'[27] In doing so, the Court has emphasised a dominant ideology of motherhood[28] that reinforces not only women's childbearing role but also their responsibility for childcare, thus conflating childbearing, which is inherently sex-specific, and childcare, which is gender-neutral. This interpretation of the exception to the equal treatment principle in Art.28(1) ETD was reiterated in a number of subsequent cases,[29] which served to both entrench women's position as primary caregivers and undermine men's access to childcare-related rights.[30] While certain

25 *Ibid*, 289–90.
26 Fredman (n.16), 121.
27 First noted in Case 184/83 *Hofmann v Barmer Ersatzkasse* [1985] ICR 731, [25].
28 Clare McGlynn, 'Ideologies of Motherhood in European Community Sex Equality Law' [2000] 6(1) ELJ 29.
29 Previously Council Directive 76/207/EEC of 9 February 1976 on the implementation of the principle of equal treatment for men and women as regards access to employment, vocational training and promotion, and working conditions, Art.2(3) (Directive 76/207). For a discussion of this jurisprudence see: *Ibid*; Eugenia Caracciolo di Torella and Annick Masselot, 'Pregnancy, Maternity and the Organisation of Family Life: An Attempt to Classify the Case Law of the Court of Justice' [2001] 26(3) EL Rev 239.
30 McGlynn (n.28); More (n.13).

decisions have begun to challenge this,[31] this ideology of motherhood has not been entirely displaced.[32] Such an interpretation of the boundaries of this exception is problematic because instead of recognising those instances when women and men should be treated equally and those where an alternative approach is justified, it extended protected beyond what was required to accommodate difference. This jurisprudence underpinned the CJEU decisions in *Z* and *CD*, prizing traditional gestational routes to parenthood to the detriment of alternatives[33] and limiting recognition of caring responsibilities thereafter.[34] These limitations were also evident in *Mayr*.

As noted in Chapter 2, the decision in *Mayr* underscored the limitations of the pregnancy discrimination framework, particularly as Art.10 PWD only prohibits dismissal during pregnancy and maternity leave and does not prohibit less favourable treatment on the grounds of pregnancy. This makes it more difficult to extend protection here to include someone undergoing ART treatments because the pre-existing pregnancy must be the reason for the dismissal.[35] This challenge was evident in the efforts made by AG Colomer to identify the point at which pregnancy begins.[36] However, the distinction between conception and implantation, while of some use to those in the latter stages of treatment, is not itself particularly helpful for those undergoing ART treatments. The route to this stage is often long. Limiting protection to this period does not adequately address the potentially vulnerable employment position of those undergoing treatment throughout the entire treatment process. Instead, a broader interpretation of the scope of pregnancy discrimination is necessary, which recognises undergoing ART treatments as a pregnancy-related condition. Doing so

---

31 (C-104/09) *Roca Alvarez v Sesa Start Espana ETT SA* [2011] 1 CMLR 28; (C-222/14) *Maistrellis v Ypourgos Dikaiosynis, Diafaneias kai Anthropinon Dikaiomaton* EU:C:2015:47; Eugenia Caracciolo di Torella, 'Brave new fathers for a brave new world? Fathers as caregivers in an evolving European Union' [2014] 20(1) Eur Law J 88; Sandra Fredman, 'Reversing Roles: Bringing Men into the Frame' [2014] 10(4) Int JLC 442.

32 (C-5/12) *Betriu Montull v Instituto Nacional de la Seguridad Social* [2014] 1 CMLR 35; Eugenia Caracciolo di Torella, 'Men in the Work/Family Reconciliation Discourse: The Swallows That Did Not Make a Summer?' [2015] 37(3) JSWFL 334.

33 Case C-363/12 *Z v A (Re Equal Treatment)* [2014] 3 CMLR 20, [AG47]-[AG49]. AG Kokott in *CD* (n.23) would have adopted a broader interpretation [AG41], but this was not followed by the CJEU.

34 Eugenia Caracciolo Di Torella and Petra Foubert, 'Surrogacy, Pregnancy and Maternity Rights: A Missed Opportunity for a More Coherent Regime of Parental Rights in the EU' [2015] EL Rev 52.

35 *Mayr* (n.4), [AG48], [41], [53].

36 *Ibid*, [AG30]–[AG38].

would require an expansive intersectional interpretation recognising the need to accommodate woman's childbearing capacity as opposed to focusing solely on the sex-specific nature of treatment.

This reinforces that in the current context, it is necessary to analyse discrimination through the overlapping lenses of gender and disability. This reflects the approach adopted for pregnancy, identified as being on the orbits of both, which recognises that pregnancy is a sex-specific circumstance requiring accommodation of difference because of its interconnection with childbearing. However, the EU has extended special protection beyond childbearing to also include childcare while at the same time limiting protections against discrimination based on the potential for pregnancy. Therefore, in attempting to redefine the boundaries of sex and/or pregnancy discrimination to include those undergoing ART treatments, it is necessary to ensure that the potential for pregnancy and the interconnection between ART treatments and childbearing capacity are acknowledged. Consequently, it is necessary to ground the analysis in sex discrimination, through the primary lens of gender, intersecting with disability insofar as it is a circumstance requiring accommodation. In these respects, it mirrors the experience and underpinning rationale of pregnancy discrimination, but it relocates the examination in the broader context of sex discrimination, which provides greater potential for redrawing the boundaries.

Sex discrimination revisited

Art.14 ETD prohibits direct and indirect discrimination on the grounds of sex in the employment context. In doing so, it adopts a symmetrical approach towards discrimination, extending protection to both women and men. However, as noted earlier, Art.28(1) provides an exception to the equal treatment principle for provisions aimed at the protection of women, particularly in relation to pregnancy and maternity. This allows for asymmetrical treatment in certain instances to ensure substantive equality. While the provision makes specific reference to pregnancy and maternity, this is not exhaustive, merely illustrative of the kinds of instances in which special treatment is permissible. Whereas the previous jurisprudence has interpreted this to reinforce traditional gender roles in relation to childcare, it is capable of being interpreted more expansively to include those undergoing ART treatments. Women undergoing treatment are in a similar position to those who are pregnant because the nature of the treatment is largely sex-specific, especially those that impact on working life, because of its inherent interconnected with childbearing capacity. This suggests that the exception in Art.28(1) retains the potential to recognise the experiences of those undergoing ART treatments and could help reinforce the distinction between sex-specific experiences requiring protection, such as childbearing, and gender-neutral childcare responsibilities which do not. These limitations, as well as the potential for expansion, are evident in the CJEU's consideration of this exception in *Mayr*.

As Vauchez suggests, the willingness of the CJEU to find some form of protection in EU law for Mayr[37] suggests an openness to recognising and accepting the vulnerable position that working women are in while undergoing ART treatments. This is evident in AG Colomer's comment on the scope of Directive 76/207 in which he states that

> even if pregnancy does not give rise to inequality based on sex, it only affects women and consequently employment-related decisions which are potentially detrimental to women and which are *motivated by pregnancy* constitute discrimination [emphasis added].[38]

The reference to 'motivated by pregnancy' has potentially far-reaching consequences and suggests that AG Colomer was envisioning that protection could extend to the pre-conception period. Thus, those undergoing ART treatments would be included because the objective is to achieve pregnancy and less favourable treatment related to this is likely to be motivated by the potential for pregnancy. Consequently, decisions that are based on undergoing ART treatments are inherently ones that are motivated by pregnancy and thus within the scope of protection. The wording also suggests that it could include childbearing potential, as in the US, and so ascriptions of stereotypical gender roles as opposed to being limited to actual pregnancy. However, the decision was much narrower. Both the AG and the CJEU held that as certain forms of ART treatment are sex-specific, discrimination against a woman because she is undergoing such treatment amounts to direct sex discrimination.[39] In doing so, the CJEU referred to the exception to the equal treatment principle and reasoned that to exclude dismissal on these grounds from the scope of protection would be contrary to the objectives underpinning it.[40] While the Court appears to adopt a broad interpretation of the exception, recognising the interconnection between childbearing capacity and sex discrimination, it is much more limited. Despite recognising

---

37 Stéphanie Hennette Vauchez, 'The Society for the Protection of Unborn Children v. Grogan: Rereading the Case and Retelling the Story of Reproductive Rights in Europe' in Nicola Fernanda and Bill Davies (eds), *EU Law Stories: Contextual and Critical Histories of European Jurisprudence* (CUP 2017) 393.
38 *Mayr* (n.4), [AG53].
39 *Ibid*, [AG68], [50].
40 *Ibid*, [51].

that some ART treatments are sex-specific, the failure to articulate the whole experience of undergoing ART treatments as inherently gendered and interconnected with childbearing capacity thus requiring accommodation results in the limited applicability of the decision in practice. This was evident in *Sahota*.[41]

The decision in *Sahota* was particularly disappointing because the EAT acknowledged that a wider interpretation, including all those undergoing ART treatments, was possible. However, concerns that such an expansive interpretation could be extended to all sex-specific conditions and treatments prevented it being adopted here.[42] Had the EAT considered the decision through the intersecting lenses of gender and disability, these concerns would have been allayed. This would have justified differential treatment based on the interconnection between this kind of sex-specific condition and the broader discriminatory treatment that women continue to face because of their childbearing potential. It is this combination of reasons that justify special protection here, not simply the fact that treatment is sex-specific. The US experience reinforces the interconnections between these considerations. This underscores the importance of adopting an alternative intersectionality approach to reinterpreting the scope of pregnancy discrimination to include those undergoing ART treatments.

Redefining the boundaries: adopting an intersectionality approach

The experiences of those engaged in ART treatments underscores both the limitations of a single ground approach and the potential for adopting an intersectionality approach. As noted earlier, the decision in *Mayr* presented the possibility of extending the boundaries of sex discrimination to include those undergoing ART treatments but was limited because of its failure to ground its reasoning in the sex-specific connection with childbearing capacity, requiring specific accommodation. Doing so would have embraced Schiek's intersecting nodes of gender and disability and the placement of pregnancy discrimination on the orbits of both, recognising its inherently intersectional character. A similar approach has been adopted in the US, which again demonstrates the potential of adopting an intersectionality approach in recognising the experiences of those undergoing ART treatments as pregnancy-related conditions.

---

41 [2010] 2 CMLR 29.
42 *Ibid*, [12].

The PDA

Prior to the enactment of the PDA, the US courts adopted a strictly symmetrical approach to sex discrimination which ignored the experiences of pregnant women.[43] In doing so, the Supreme Court focused on the question of whether the treatment was the same,[44] without any consideration of the experience of childbearing. While dissenting opinions did recognise the impact of pregnancy on work,[45] they did not specifically frame their reasoning in terms of childbearing capacity, focusing instead on the sex-specific experiences. These decisions led to the enactment of the PDA, which amended Title VII of the Civil Rights Act 1964 (CRA), extending sex discrimination to include 'pregnancy, childbirth, or related medical conditions.'[46] In doing so, Bentley argues the PDA amendment recognised the asymmetrical experiences of women relating to childbearing capacity and the need to recognise and accommodate such difference to achieve equality, particularly for working women. Thus, the protection enables women to combine having a family while remaining in work in the same way as has always been the case for men.[47]

In extending protection, the aim of Congress was to define sex discrimination broadly to include the whole process of childbearing, including protecting women from discrimination based solely on the potential for pregnancy.[48] This understanding of the parameters of protection is much broader than that in the EU, and the UK, and suggests an openness to interpreting the boundaries of protection expansively to include not only stereotypes regarding appropriate gender roles but also the specific experiences of those undergoing ART treatments. However, the PDA remains underpinned by formal equality,[49] only extending the same rights that are available to other temporarily disabled workers to pregnant workers. Consequently, the effect of the legislation was merely to extend the equal treatment provisions of Title VII to the sex-specific childbearing experience, without enacting further rights or protections. Despite these shortcomings,

43 *Geduldig v Aiello et al.* 417 US 484 (1973); *General Electric Company v Gilbert et al.* 429 US 125 (1978).
44 *Geduldig* (n.43), 496–97; *Gilbert* (n.43), 137–40.
45 Brennan J delivered the dissenting opinions in both cases: *Geduldig* (n.43), 497–505; *Gilbert* (n.43), 146–60.
46 CRA, §701(k) (2000e(k) as codified) inserted by the PDA, s.1.
47 Bentley (n.21), 403.
48 As discussed *ibid*, 403–5.
49 Michelle D. Deardorff, 'Beyond Pregnancy: Litigating Infertility, Contraception, and Breastfeeding in the Workplace' [2011] 32(1) Journal of Women, Politics & Policy 52, 54–55.

the PDA offers the potential for a broader interpretation of the instances when protection is afforded. By recognising the interrelationship between the sex-specific experiences of childbearing and the need to accommodate it, thus embodying the intersections between gender and disability, it has the potential to include those undergoing ART treatments as pregnancy-related conditions.

From 'a related medical condition' to a focus on childbearing capacity

There are two opposing lines of authority regarding whether those undergoing ART treatments are included within the scope of the PDA.[50] One focuses on infertility as a gender-neutral condition and thus excludes it from the scope of sex and pregnancy-related discrimination. The other recognises the sex-specific experience of undergoing treatment and accepts that it is a pregnancy-related medical condition, moving towards articulating this in terms of childbearing capacity. The first case to address this was *Pacourek*,[51] in which the plaintiff argued that infertility was a pregnancy-related medical condition, thus within the scope of the PDA.[52] Pacourek argued that her employer's application of their sick leave policy was discriminatory and to her detriment when she was ultimately dismissed. Her employer was aware that her absences were related to undergoing IVF treatment, and she had evidence confirming this. In response, the employers argued that the inability to become pregnant is not a pregnancy-related condition and that infertility is a gender-neutral condition, meaning that her status is not a uniquely female one; thus, the PDA does not apply.[53]

In determining the claims, the District Court decided that the first issue was whether the PDA covered potential or intended pregnancy, which the Court reasoned it did. In doing so, it referred to the purpose of the PDA and the circumstances in which it was enacted,[54] noting,

> The basic theory of the PDA may be simply stated: Only women can become pregnant; stereotypes based on pregnancy and related medical

---

50 For a discussion see: Deardorff (n.49); Katie Cushing, 'Facing Reality: The Pregnancy Discrimination Act Falls Short for Women Undergoing Infertility Treatment' [2010] 40 Seton Hall Law Review 1697.
51 *Pacourek* (n.5); affirmed in *Pacourek v Inland Steel Company* 916 F.Supp.797 (ND Ill 1996).
52 *Pacourek* (n.5), 1400–1.
53 *Ibid*, 1401.
54 *Ibid*, 1401–2.

conditions have been a barrier to women's economic advancement; and classifications based on pregnancy and related medical conditions are never gender-neutral. Discrimination against an employee because she intends to, is trying to, or simply has the potential to become pregnant is therefore illegal discrimination.[55]

Such reasoning reinforces the need to overcome ascriptions based on stereotypical gender roles relating to childbearing capacity, as well as the specific experiences of those undergoing ART treatments. This reasoning was supported by the Supreme Court decision, *International Union, UAW v Johnson Controls, Inc.*,[56] in which the Court held that the employer's policy of excluding only fertile women from work that could adversely affect their fertility and/or unborn foetus amounted to sex discrimination prohibited by Title VII.[57] In reaching this decision, the Court acknowledged that risks to fertility were gender-neutral; however, the aim of the policy here was gender-specific since it singled out women with childbearing capacity.[58] In doing so, the Court recognised the inherent tensions and stereotypes that all women are exposed to because of their childbearing capacity, irrespective of whether they have children.[59] The reasoning here is reflective of Schiek's intersecting nodes approach because it recognises the inherently gendered experience of childbearing as a whole, not just during the limited period of pregnancy but also, more generally, underpinning stereotypes regarding gender roles and the need to accommodate that difference when women are actually engaged in it. In doing so, this reasoning is sufficiently broad to also encompass those undergoing ART treatments as an intended pregnancy, because women similarly experience stereotyping and barriers to economic advancement while undergoing treatment.

Turning to the second issue of whether her condition was a pregnancy-related medical condition the Court noted that the language of the PDA was sufficiently broad to allow for an expansive interpretation of its scope and was capable of including infertility as a pregnancy-related medical condition.[60] The Court reinforced that the consequence of this was not that her employer had to treat her in a more favourable way, just that her

---

55 *Ibid*, 1401.
56 499 US 187, (1991).
57 *Johnson Controls* (n.56), 197–200.
58 *Ibid*, 199.
59 Judith G. Greenberg, 'The Pregnancy Discrimination Act: Legitimating Discrimination Against Pregnant Women in the Workforce' [1998] 50(2) Me L Rev 225, 231–32.
60 *Pacourek* (n.5), 1402–3.

pregnancy-related condition be treated in a neutral way.[61] This meant that her fertility treatment-related absences should be ignored when applying absence management policies. Furthermore, as noted in Chapter 3, the Court rejected the employer's argument that infertility affects both men and women in the same way.[62] Instead, it held that accepting that reasoning would undermine the purpose of the legislation, which is aimed at alleviating such apparently gender-neutral provisions which impose greater burdens on women in practice.[63] In doing so, this interpretation of the legislation appears to implicitly endorse Schiek's intersectionality approach by recognising and addressing the inherent stereotypes and barriers to women's engagement that are rooted in reproductive capacity while also recognising the need to accommodate difference when appropriate. This decision was later affirmed in *Erickson*.[64]

However, in *Krauel v Iowa Methodist Medical Center*,[65] the plaintiff's similar argument that the exclusion of certain ART treatments from medical insurance coverage amounted to less favourable treatment on the grounds of a pregnancy-related medical condition contrary to the PDA was rejected. Unlike in *Pacourek*, the question of whether fertility treatment and potential pregnancy were covered by the PDA was separated from the initial question of whether infertility treatment amounted to treatment for pregnancy or a related medical condition.[66] In doing so, the District Court failed to consider whether infertility was covered itself or as a pregnancy-related condition.[67] Instead, the Court reasoned that ART treatments were not analogous with pregnancy or childbirth, which refer to the post-conception period, since they are undertaken in the pre-conception period.[68] Furthermore, the Court reasoned that infertility affects both women and men and so is not gender-specific. In reaching this conclusion, it distinguished the approach adopted in *Pacourek*[69] and ignored the legislative history of the PDA.[70] Moreover, in the disparate impact analysis,[71] the Court dismissed Krauel's arguments that women bear the greatest

---

61 *Ibid*, 1403.
62 The separate issue of whether infertility is gender-neutral was not properly put before the Court, and so was not considered.
63 *Pacourek* (n.5), 1403–4.
64 *Erickson* (n.5), 318–20.
65 915 F.Supp.102 (SD Iowa 1995).
66 *Ibid*, 111–13.
67 Bentley (n.21), 414.
68 *Krauel* (n.65), 112.
69 *Ibid*, 112–13.
70 Bentley (n.21), 414–15.
71 Indirect discrimination in the UK context.

burdens of the impact of treatment as well as its costs. Instead, it noted that these are medical not employment issues and so are irrelevant in this context, reinforcing the boundaries between public and private spheres.[72] In doing so, the Court failed to adequately consider the impact of undergoing treatment on employment, which is primarily, if not exclusively, borne by women. Nevertheless, this was upheld on appeal.[73] This decision reinforces the significance of the interconnection between acknowledging the sex-specific experiences of undergoing treatment and protection being afforded here. When the Court fails to adopt this preliminary analysis of the lived experiences of infertility,[74] it also fails to extend protection because it disregards the connection with childbearing capacity. This reinforces the importance of adopting an intersectionality analysis when interpreting the boundaries of protection here. This is underscored in the decision in *Saks v Franklin Covey*.[75]

In *Saks*, what appeared to be a step forward for those seeking access to treatment was quickly dashed by the District Court. While it was accepted that infertility was a pregnancy-related medical condition,[76] the Court also held that the plan did not amount to prohibited sex discrimination contrary to Title VII CRA. While both women and men received the same benefits and exclusions under the plan, all infertility treatments available to men were covered, but this was not the case for women with all surgical implantation procedures explicitly excluded.[77] The presumption that the plan was not discriminatory since it was applied equally is inherently problematic, because it fails to recognise the particular implications for working women with fertility issues. This was upheld on appeal to the 2nd Circuit COA.[78] In this instance, the comparison between male and female infertility fails to adequately recognise the different burdens and treatments involved, which impact most significantly on women because of their childbearing capacity. The Courts determined that there was no difference based on sex because the partners of male employees were equally excluded from coverage.[79] However, this still fails to acknowledge that it is only treatment undertaken by women that is specifically excluded from its scope. As in *Krauel*, the Courts separated the issue of infertility from ART treatments, thus

72 *Krauel* (n.65), 114. Greenberg (n.59), 232.
73 *Krauel v Iowa Methodist Medical Center*, 95 F.3d 674, 680–81.
74 Bentley (n.21), 416–17; Cushing (n.50), 1717–19.
75 117 F.Supp.2d 318 (SDNY 2000).
76 *Ibid*, 328–29.
77 *Ibid*, 328.
78 *Saks v Franklin Covey* 316 F.3d 337 (2003).
79 *Ibid*, 344–45 affirming *Saks* (n.75), 328–29.

preventing an adequate analysis of the gendered experience of infertility and undergoing treatment.[80] The reasoning adopted by the Court is difficult to reconcile with both the earlier decisions and its own decision to recognise infertility as a pregnancy-related medical condition. What it again demonstrates is the shortcomings of analysing this experience through one equality lens. By focusing solely on pregnancy-related discrimination here, the Court recognised that in principle, it should be included within the scope of protection. However, by failing to recognise that access to treatment has sex-specific consequences, particularly for women, this initial acceptance is rendered meaningless in practice. It is only by adopting an intersectionality analysis that effective protection is afforded. This underscores the problem of treating infertility as a gender-neutral medical condition, and ART treatments like any other kind of sex-specific treatment. Doing so ignores the gendered aspect of undergoing treatment and its inherent connection with pregnancy and/or childbearing capacity.[81] However, this reasoning was subsequently followed in *LaPorta v Wal-Mart Stores, Inc.*, which held that there was nothing to suggest that the PDA had intended to cover infertility as a pregnancy-related condition.[82]

Nevertheless, the issue arose again in *Hall v Nalco Co.*, in which the plaintiff claimed that she had been selected for dismissal because she had undergone multiple rounds of IVF treatment.[83] Hall claimed that this amounted to sex discrimination in relation to her intention to become pregnant through fertility treatments.[84] The 7th Circuit COA held that she had a cognisable claim under the PDA,[85] focusing on the sex-specific nature of the treatment and its consequences for women. The Court reinforced that discrimination based on pregnancy, and related medical conditions, is inherently discrimination because of sex.[86] It recognised that the consequences of infertility are different for women and men, and changed the narrative from the question of whether infertility is gender-neutral, which it conceded it was, to focus instead on childbearing capacity.[87] In

---

80 Cushing (n.50), 1719–20.

81 Bentley (n.21), 415–19.

82 163 F.Supp.2d 758 (WD Mich 2001), 770–71.

83 *Hall* (n.5), 645–46.

84 Unlike most other cases, the applicability of the ADA was not considered here, representing a missed opportunity to re-examine protection here: Kerry Van der Burch, 'Courts' Struggle with Infertility: The Impact of *Hall v. Nalco* on Infertility-Related Employment Discrimination' [2010] 81 University of Colorado L Rev 545, 571–75.

85 While the Court did not determine the merits of the case, its analysis of the presented facts suggest that it would have upheld her claim on its merits too: *Hall* (n.5), 649.

86 *Ibid*, 647.

87 *Ibid*, 648–49.

doing so, the Court referred again to the decision in *Johnson Controls* in relation to potential pregnancy and acknowledged the inherently gendered consequences of reproduction, in general, as well as in the specific context of undergoing ART treatments. Consequently, they held that decisions relating to childbearing capacity only affect women and so fall within the scope of discrimination under the PDA.[88]

While the decision moves away from the question of whether infertility is sex-specific and/or is a pregnancy-related medical condition, it reinforces the underlying purpose of that consideration, namely that infertility and undergoing ART treatments have sex-specific consequences that are inherently linked with women's childbearing capacity, and so are pregnancy-related.[89] Indeed, such an approach is beneficial for those undergoing ART treatments because focusing on the sex-specific nature of treatment alone is always potentially vulnerable to a symmetrical treatment analysis. Grounding the reasoning in childbearing capacity instead removes this by focusing on the inherently unique experience of childbearing, which requires accommodation, and is not analogous with any male experience. Indeed, the move away from focusing on the gendered nature of infertility benefits those undergoing ART treatments for other reasons while still recognising the inherently gendered experiences and burdens faced by women in this context. Although the Court was criticised for not explicitly stating that childbearing capacity was the reason for its decision, as opposed to the sex-specific nature of the treatment itself. It has been argued that a disparate impact (indirect discrimination) analysis would have been better able to address these issues and ensure that the decision is followed correctly in future.[90] However, adopting such an approach allows for justifications, which would limit protection in practice. Nevertheless, the decision again reinforces the interrelationship between gender and disability in the sense of accommodating difference. Although it is still limited by the underpinning legislative framework, which remains rooted in a formal equality approach, and thus only requires equal, rather than more favourable, treatment.[91]

The US jurisprudence reinforces the importance of recognising the inherently gendered experience of undergoing ART treatments because of its connection with childbearing capacity and its implications for workplace

---

88 *Ibid*, 645, discussed further at 649.
89 Bentley (n.21), 416–19; Cushing (n.50), 1717.
90 Recent Cases Employment Law – Title VII – Seventh Circuit Allows Employee Terminated for Undergoing in Vitro Fertilization to Bring Sex Discrimination Claim. – Hall v. Nalco Co., 534 F.3d 644 (7th Cir. 2008) [2009] 122(5) Harvard L R 1533, 1536, 1538–40; Van der Burch (n.84), 566–70.
91 Cushing (n.50), 1720–22.

engagement. This requires the courts to view this experience through the intersecting lenses of gender and disability, understanding and valuing this experience, to ensure that the equality aims underpinning the legislation are fulfilled in practice.[92] This again demonstrates the importance of adopting an intersectional analysis to effectively include the experiences of those undergoing ART treatments within its scope. While the underpinning legislative framework also allowed greater potential for reinterpretation than that in the EU, it nevertheless reinforces the significance of intersectionality as an analytical tool in broadening its scope.

Redefining pregnancy-related discrimination in the UK

The foregoing has again demonstrated that adopting an intersectionality approach, this time around the primary node of gender intersecting with disability, can facilitate a broader understanding of protected characteristics to include those undergoing ART treatments. Drawing from this experience, and Schiek's intersecting nodes, UK law is re-examined to determine whether the boundaries can be redefined to include pregnancy-related discrimination. The limitations of the pregnancy discrimination provisions are examined first before considering the potential to broaden the parameters of sex discrimination. Comparisons are drawn with attempts to extend associative discrimination to include direct sex discrimination on the grounds of someone else's pregnancy. This suggests that the boundaries of protection can be drawn more broadly and could include those engaged in ART treatments within its scope.

Reinterpreting pregnancy

The interrelationship between childbearing capacity and gender in the UK is recognised in the specific protected characteristic of pregnancy, defined in s.18(2) EqA as prohibiting pregnancy discrimination

> against a woman if, in the protected period in relation to a pregnancy of *hers*, A treats her unfavourably (a) because of the pregnancy, or (b) because of illness suffered by her as a result of it [emphasis added].

The interconnection between protection and pregnancy is further underscored in s.18(6), which states that protection starts when pregnancy

---

92 Bentley (n.21), 415–22.

begins. These provisions, like those in the EU, pose interpretative problems for those undergoing ART treatments. They draw clear distinctions between those already pregnant, who are afforded protection, and those undergoing ART treatments, who would not be included until pregnancy begins. This is equally true of pregnancy-related illnesses, which are limited to those deriving from pregnancy, as opposed to more broadly relating to those having an impact on childbearing capacity or potential pregnancy, as in the US. The reasoning adopted in the EU context for excluding those undergoing treatment from protection is likely to be mirrored here. While pregnancy, in principle, offers the most suitable conceptual framework for extending protection here, the wording of the provisions in the EqA limits this potential in practice. This indicates that in order to recognise the lived experiences of those undergoing ART treatments, one of two options is necessary. Specific amendments could be made to the EqA to include those undergoing treatments, such as reframing pregnancy-related illness as a pregnancy-related condition, which includes both infertility and undergoing ART treatments. Doing so would recognise the inherent interconnection between undergoing ART treatments and their potential for pregnancy. Thus, analysing the experience through the intersecting lenses of sex and disability enables childbearing capacity to be acknowledged and accommodated. Alternatively, and possibly more likely, is returning to reconceptualising pregnancy, including pregnancy-related issues, as a form of direct sex discrimination, thus removing the requirement for a pre-existing pregnancy as a precursor to extending protection.

Sex is expressed in s.11 in symmetrical terms, extending protection to both women and men, which poses potential problems if a symmetrical approach is adopted here. Since asymmetrical pregnancy protection is addressed separately in s.18, it poses the question of whether discrimination on the grounds of pregnancy and/or childbearing capacity could fall within the parameters of direct sex discrimination under s.13. Section 18(7) refers to the interaction between these provisions and states that s.13 does not apply to the treatment of a woman in the protected period of pregnancy or because of a pregnancy-related illness or during maternity leave. Furthermore, s.13(6)(b) makes it clear that men cannot claim direct sex discrimination with respect to special treatment given to women in relation to pregnancy and maternity.[93] Nevertheless, it does not preclude less favourable treatment on the grounds of pregnancy, pregnancy-related

---

93 As seen in the joined cases on statutory shared parental leave pay: *Ali v Capita Customer Management Ltd* and *Chief Constable of Leicestershire Police v Hextall* [2019] EWCA Civ 900, 2019 WL 02256085.

illness and maternity leave from still being considered forms of direct sex discrimination. This would enable the experiences of those undergoing treatment to be examined through the intersecting lenses of gender and disability, as in pregnancy but without its limitations. Consequently, reinterpreting the scope of direct sex discrimination to include less favourable treatment on pregnancy-related grounds, such as childbearing capacity, could be extended to encompass those engaged in ART treatments. This would be consistent with the approach adopted in *Mayr* but would extend it to instead focus on childbearing capacity as in the US. Recognising pregnancy and/or childbearing capacity as a form of direct sex discrimination offers greater interpretative potential. However, it would still require a broad interpretation to be adopted, recognising that 'on the grounds of sex' can include (potential) pregnancy and/or childbearing capacity. This potential has been tested in cases of associative pregnancy discrimination.

Associative pregnancy discrimination

The potential for sex discrimination to be interpreted more expansively was raised in the context of attempts to extend associative discrimination, as recognised in (C-303/06) *Coleman v Attridge Law (A Firm)*,[94] to pregnancy. In *Coleman*, the CJEU interpreted the equal treatment principle embodied in the FWD broadly to include those who were discriminated against on one of the protected grounds, in that case disability, irrespective of whether they themselves had that characteristic.[95] In doing so, the Court reasoned that as the purpose of the FWD was to create 'a level playing field as regards equality in employment and occupation,'[96] this could only be achieved by adopting such a broad interpretation. The CJEU focused on the wording of the directive which referred to grounds rather than categories of people, meaning protection was afforded when someone was discriminated against on one of the protected grounds rather than because they had that characteristic.[97]

---

94 [2008] ECR I-5603. Fredman (n.10), argues that the decision adopts a capacious interpretation of disability, reflecting an intersectionality approach with disability intersecting with gender, 77–78.

95 *Ibid*, [43]–[51], [56]. Council Directive 2000/78/EC of 27 November 2000 establishing a general framework for equal treatment in employment and occupation.

96 *Ibid*, [47].

97 This was followed by the UK EAT in its subsequent interpretation of the Disability Discrimination Act 1995: *EBR Attridge Law LLP (formerly Attridge Law) v Coleman* [2010] 1 CMLR 28, [14]–[16].

The question of whether this could extend to pregnancy was subsequently raised in the Scottish case, *Kulikaoskas*. Both the claimant and his partner worked for the same employer, and both were dismissed after he had been caught moving heavy boxes for her because she was pregnant. Kulikaoskas claimed that he had been discriminated against on the grounds of pregnancy under the Sex Discrimination Act 1975 s.3A(1) (now s.18(1) EqA), with reference to *Coleman* and associative discrimination.[98] Lady Smith in the EAT first noted that associative discrimination was not included within the scope of s.3A on a plain reading of the text.[99] While this may have been true, the examples given to illustrate this point are problematic. Lady Smith refers to a teacher dismissed for getting a pupil pregnant and a priest dismissed for getting a nun pregnant. She argues that in each case, dismissal would be on the grounds of pregnancy, which would amount to prohibited direct sex discrimination. However, the reasons for dismissal in these examples is not the pregnancy per se but the inappropriate sexual relationship, which would amount to gross misconduct and be a fair reason for dismissal.[100] A female teacher would similarly be fairly dismissed if she was pregnant with a pupil's child because of the inappropriate sexual relationship and not the pregnancy as such. This reinforces that the reason for the discrimination is key here rather than the mere presence of pregnancy itself, which is reflected in the automatically unfair dismissal provisions themselves.[101]

Nevertheless, Lady Smith further distinguished *Coleman* on the grounds that it was decided under the FWD and a different approach should be taken for pregnancy with reference to the PWD and the ETD.[102] Indeed, in *CD* when AG Kokott considered whether the commissioning mother was subject to less favourable treatment based on her association with the surrogate she referred only to the PWD. However, as discrimination was limited to those who are or have been pregnant, it could not extend to commissioning mothers.[103] Lady Smith examined the relevant provisions in the ETD and reasoned that the specific reference to women in Art.2(2)(c), rather than person as in Arts.2(2)(a)–(b), suggested that only pregnant women were envisaged here.[104] Furthermore, this was considered consistent with previous approaches, which protected pregnant women from

---

98 *Kulikaoskas* (n.6), [20]–[27].

99 *Ibid*, [32].

100 Employment Rights Act 1996, s.98(2)(b).

101 *Ibid*, s.99, wherein it prohibits dismissal where pregnancy (among other things) is the reason or principal reason for dismissal.

102 *Kulikaoskas* (n.6), [37].

103 *CD* (n.23), [AG83]–[AG88].

104 *Kulikaoskas* (n.6), [37].

harms,[105] as opposed to wider risks of unequal treatment. In reaching this conclusion, Lady Smith referred to the jurisprudence which focused only on physical and mental risks[106] rather than stereotypical and societal barriers facing pregnant workers and, more generally, women of childbearing age.

While this decision appeared to suggest that associative discrimination could not be extended to pregnancy-related discrimination, the decision was appealed to the Court of Session (CoS), which referred two questions to the CJEU. These sought to clarify whether less favourable treatment on the grounds of a woman's pregnancy was within the scope of the ETD and whether it would apply to the partner of a pregnant woman or persons otherwise associated with a pregnant woman.[107] Effectively, these questions sought to determine whether the decision in *Coleman* could be extended to the interpretation of the ETD. The answers to these questions would have had significant implications, not only for the partners of pregnant women but also potentially for commissioning parents, who could be interpreted as being otherwise associated with a pregnant woman. However, the case was settled prior to the hearing.[108] Consequently, the question of whether the ETD should be interpreted more broadly and consistently with the decision in *Coleman* remains unknown. Nevertheless, the issue was subsequently considered by another Scottish tribunal in *Gyenes*.

In *Gyenes* the claimants, a married couple, argued that they had been dismissed because of the wife's pregnancy. Their employer purported to 'permanently lay them' off shortly after discovering that Mrs Gyenes was pregnant.[109] They were the only ones laid off, and as there was no evidence to suggest that this reason was genuine,[110] the ET had no difficulty in determining that the real reason for dismissal was pregnancy.[111] The ET then considered whether Mr Gyenes could have been discriminated against on the grounds of his wife's pregnancy. The ET reasoned that s.18 did not allow pregnancy association claims given its specific reference to the pregnant woman. This reflects the interpretation of s.18 discussed earlier, and the approach adopted by AG Kokott in *CD*, and was not unexpected here. Consequently, the ET turned its consideration to whether it fell within the

---

105 *Ibid*, [34], [37].
106 *Ibid*, [34].
107 Case C-44/12: Reference for a preliminary ruling from Court of Session (Scotland), Edinburgh (United Kingdom) made on 30 January 2012.
108 OJ C 108, 13 April 2013, p. 18.
109 *Gyenes* (n.6), [17]. A concept unknown to the ET and UK employment law.
110 *Ibid*, [25]–[35].
111 *Ibid*, [36]–[42].

scope of direct sex discrimination under s.13.[112] Reflecting the alternative approach to extending pregnancy, and pregnancy-related protection, suggested earlier. Thus, presenting the opportunity to reinterpret the scope of sex discrimination, with potentially wider implications, including for those undergoing ART treatments. Before doing so, the ET reflected upon the decision in *Kulikaoskas* and its attempt to apply the reasoning in *Coleman*. While acknowledging that the case had been unsuccessful in the EAT, the ET focused on the different approach taken by the CoS[113] and examined whether it could fall within the scope of direct sex discrimination under s.13(1).[114] The ET also found support for this in the Equality and Human Rights Commission (EHRC) Employment Code,[115] which suggested that less favourable treatment because of an association with pregnancy could amount to direct sex discrimination.[116] It also reasoned that this was consistent with the decision in *Coleman*.[117] In particular, the ET held that there was no reason why a less robust conception of equality was justified for pregnant women as compared with disability or other protected groups.[118] Finally, the ET reasoned that pregnancy discrimination is a form of direct discrimination on the grounds of sex. Since Art.2(1)(a) ETD includes 'treatment on the grounds of sex', it reasoned this was sufficiently broad enough to include another person's sex.[119] Unlike the EAT in *Kulikaoskas*, it disagreed that the reference to a woman in Art.2(2)(c) precluded associative discrimination here.[120] Nevertheless, the ET was careful to frame the claim as one of sex, rather than pregnancy, discrimination. While this requires a comparator, the ET had no trouble identifying a hypothetical comparator who did the same job but was not associated with a pregnant woman and reasoned that such a comparator would not have been treated less favourably.[121] Thus, the ET held that he was directly discriminated on the grounds of sex because of his wife's pregnancy.[122] In doing so, it presented an alternative interpretation of the boundaries of sex discrimination, one which could have significant implications for those engaged in ART treatments.

112 *Ibid*, [44].
113 *Ibid*, [45]–[46].
114 *Ibid*, [49].
115 Equality and Human Rights Commission, *Equality Act 2010: Employment Statutory Code of Practice* (EHRC 2011) 3.18.
116 *Gyenes* (n.6), [50].
117 *Ibid*, [51]–[52].
118 *Ibid*, [55]–[56].
119 *Ibid*, [53].
120 *Ibid*, [54].
121 *Ibid*, [57].
122 *Ibid*, [58].

Recognising less favourable treatment on the grounds of someone else's pregnancy presents the opportunity for commissioning mothers, and fathers, to argue that they have been discriminated against on the grounds of the surrogate's pregnancy. This could encompass less favourable treatment in terms of access to work-family rights, including time off to attend ART treatments and other appointments. While they may not be in a relationship of care, unlike partners of pregnant women, they have a closely interdependent relationship which is rooted in pregnancy. Being able to extend associative discrimination to commissioning parents would recognise the interdependency of this relationship. It is less clear whether this decision and reasoning could equally extend to those undergoing ART treatments. Insofar as this concept of discrimination relates solely to direct sex discrimination because of pregnancy, it is difficult to reconcile this with those who are not yet pregnant, particularly if the same definition of pregnancy as in s.18 is adopted here. However, if a 'robust conception of equality'[123] is necessary to ensure that protected characteristics are fully protected in practice, then such a broad conception of equality should be wide enough to instead frame this in terms of childbearing capacity as a form of direct sex discrimination. In doing so, it would reflect the intersectional analysis inherent in pregnancy discrimination and similarly view the experiences of all those engaged in ART treatments through the intersecting lenses of gender and disability.

However, it is important to bear in mind that *Geynes* was only a first-instance decision, and neither the employer nor its representatives attended the hearing. Nevertheless, it indicates that there is some willingness to interpret the boundaries of protection more broadly. The ET achieved this by considering the overlapping nature of the protected characteristics of sex and pregnancy and the wider equality principle, as well as the desire to make some accommodations because of the unique characteristics of pregnancy. Analogous arguments can be made for extending this reasoning to pregnancy-related discrimination and/or childbearing capacity, thus recognising the experiences of those undergoing ART treatments. If the underpinning rationale is to prevent less favourable treatment because of the impact of childbearing on women's workplace engagement, then this is equally relevant in this context.

These efforts by the Scottish courts to redefine these boundaries and embrace a more robust conceptualisation of equality indicates a willingness to redraw these lines to encompass undesirable treatment within its scope. Doing so requires going back to the beginning and recognising pregnancy

---

123 *Ibid*, [56].

as an inherent form of direct sex discrimination, requiring accommodation of difference. This involves analysing the experiences and legislation through the intersecting lenses of gender and disability to recognise childbearing capacity and the experience of undergoing ART treatments as inherently gendered and requiring accommodation of difference. This is consistent with the approach adopted in the US jurisprudence recognising ART treatments within the scope of pregnancy-related discrimination and could suggest a similar interpretative potential here. This would draw from the original decision in *Mayr*, but instead of focusing on the sex-specific nature of treatment alone, it acknowledges the interrelationship with childbearing capacity, thus facilitating a similar extension of protection here.

Conclusion

The analysis in this chapter demonstrates that adopting an intersectionality approach, this time through the primary lens of gender intersecting with disability, could enable the boundaries of pregnancy and/or sex discrimination to be redrawn to include those undergoing ART treatments. This is evident in the US context, particularly in those cases which recognise the gendered aspects of undergoing treatment because of the interconnection with childbearing capacity. However, the analysis also demonstrates the limitations of the current EU and UK legal frameworks, particularly given the lack of internal mechanisms to facilitate such a reinterpretation in the first instance, unlike in the context of disability. The specific protection afforded for pregnancy discrimination makes it extremely difficult to extend the boundaries to include those who are not yet pregnant. This is particularly frustrating because the asymmetrical approach adopted in pregnancy discrimination would have been appropriate for those undergoing treatment given that the experiences and underpinning rationales are analogous. However, re-examining sex discrimination through the intersecting lenses of gender and disability offers a much greater potential to reinterpret the parameters of protection. Doing so recognises that it is the capacity for childbearing, which is inherently linked with pregnancy, that requires accommodation here. This is much broader than the approach adopted in *Mayr*, which focuses solely on the gendered nature of treatment. This analysis demonstrates that recognising childbearing capacity as an inherent form of direct sex discrimination through the intersecting lenses of gender and disability is necessary to continue to extend protection to those undergoing ART treatments throughout the treatment period.

5 A right to time off work to undergo ART treatments

Introduction

In this chapter, it is argued that the current limitations of UK equality law protection are only one facet of the problem facing those undergoing ART treatments and that specific employment rights are also necessary. In particular, the absence of a specific right to time off work enabling employees to undergo ART treatments leaves them vulnerable to dismissal and/or less favourable treatment.[1] This is particularly the case if a reinterpretation of the scope of equality law cannot be achieved but is equally important alongside this. The gaps in the current employment law framework concerning rights to time off work are examined first. This shows that while those undergoing ART treatments are excluded from many of these rights, there are already frameworks in place that could either be extended to include those undergoing ART treatments or be used as a model to develop new rights. Comparisons are again drawn with the experience in the US and the right to medical leave under the Family and Medical Leave Act 1993 (FMLA).[2] While the FMLA does not necessarily offer a right to leave for those involved in ART treatments in the US,[3] the legal framework is used as a model which can be modified in the UK context. Drawing from this, two alternatives are considered, namely a specific right to paid time off work to undergo ART treatments and a more general right to flexible, paid medical leave. Given the challenges of undergoing treatment and the desire of many to keep this private, it is acknowledged that the right to medical leave may be more realistic in practice. However, more specific rights

---

1 As was argued in *Sahota v The Home Office* [2010] 2 CMLR 29, [3].
2 Public Law 103–3.
3 Katie Cushing, 'Facing Reality: The Pregnancy Discrimination Act Falls Short for Women Undergoing Infertility Treatment' [2010] 40 Seton Hall Law Review 1697, 1725–26.

would be preferable to recognise the increasing normalisation of treatment and reduce the stigma and burdens many of those undergoing treatment face. Consequently, the possibility of more specific rights is envisaged for the future.

Combining work and ART treatment: without a legal framework

The cases involving those undergoing ART treatments have highlighted the vulnerability of the employment security of those undergoing treatment because of the lack of a legal framework enabling them to combine treatment with work. While individuals have made use of statutory and/ or employer rights to sick leave and pay, where it is provided, the cases discussed previously underscored that these frameworks have proved insufficient on their own. In the UK context, guidance from both the EHRC and ACAS reinforce that there is no clear legal framework here.[4] While employers are encouraged to act sympathetically to employees engaged in treatment,[5] employer responses are varied in practice,[6] leaving those undergoing treatment without any clear guidance on how treatment may impact on their employment security. There are several rights that either do or could be extended to those undergoing ART treatments. These include the right to statutory sick pay (SSP), the right to request flexible working and rights to time off during the ante-natal period.

SSP

The right to SSP does not afford employees with a specific right to time off work to attend appointments and/or undergo treatment. Instead, the right is framed as a right to wage replacement while the employee is unable to work because of a verified medical reason. Under the Social Security Contributions and Benefits Act 1992 (SSCBA), s.151(4) limits the instances when SSP is paid in respect of a day of incapacity for work, meaning that he or she is unable to do reasonably expected work because of illness or

---

4 Equality and Human Rights Commission (EHRC), *Equality Act 2010: Employment Statutory Code of Practice* (EHRC 2011) 8.44, 17.28–17.29; ACAS (Advice, Conciliation and Arbitration Service), Employees' Rights during IVF Treatment <www.acas. org.uk/index.aspx?articleid=5457> accessed 30 July 2019.
5 *Ibid.*
6 Nicola Payne, Susan Seenan and Olga van den Akker, 'Experiences and Psychological Distress of Fertility Treatment and Employment' [2019] 40(2) Journal of Psychosomatic Obstetrics & Gynecology 156, 159–60.

disablement. While it is entirely possible to conceptualise infertility and/or undergoing ART treatment as a physical disablement, as argued in Chapter 3, the requirement that it render the individual incapable of doing the work they are contracted to do could be more difficult to satisfy. When the individual is undergoing specific treatments, it is more likely that this could be satisfied, but other appointments may not be as easily included within this definition. The application of SSP is also limited in practice because it requires a minimum period of four consecutive days of incapacity before it is engaged.[7] Given that the treatment necessitating absence from work often occurs over a discontinuous but concentrated period, it is unlikely that it will always satisfy the requirement of consecutive days of incapacity required here. It must also fall within a period of entitlement, which begins when the period of incapacity begins and ends: when that period ends, when the entitlement to SSP ends, when the contract ends or, if in the case of a pregnant employee, when the disqualifying period begins.[8] However, if there are two periods of incapacity for the same reason, within an eight-week period, this will be treated as a single period of incapacity,[9] meaning that there is no requirement for an additional three-day waiting period. This could be useful for those undergoing treatments, if the first period of incapacity met the requirements. It must also be a qualifying day, meaning a day in which they are required to work,[10] and they must earn more than the lower earnings limit.[11] The maximum amount of SSP is 28 weeks' pay in any three-year period,[12] which is capped at the statutory amount currently £94.25.[13] The maximum period of leave may be challenging for those undergoing multiple cycles of treatment, particularly alongside ordinary sickness absences.

While these provisions allow for payments to be made while an employee is absent from work, they provide no right to time off work and no protections against detriments and/or dismissal while doing so. Consequently, an individual remains vulnerable to dismissal for absences from work as a potentially fair reason for dismissal under the Employment Rights Act 1996 (ERA). Periods of absence could be used to justify dismissal on the grounds of capability, relating to ill health, or conduct,[14] which is particu-

---

7 SSCBA, s.152(2) and s.155(1).
8 *Ibid*, s.153(1)–(2).
9 *Ibid*, s.152(3).
10 *Ibid*, s.154.
11 *Ibid*, sch.11, para.2 and s.5(1)(a).
12 *Ibid*, s.155(4).
13 *Ibid*, s.157.
14 *Ibid*, s.98(2)(a)–(b).

larly likely where there is a persistent level of short-term absences from work, often with little notice, as would be the case for those undergoing ART treatments. However, an employer must still consider the employee's situation and reasons for absence as well as provide warnings, as appropriate, that continued absences could result in dismissal.[15] Nevertheless, the lack of specific rights to time off work to undergo treatment leaves employees vulnerable to dismissal, and/or having to choose to forgo ART treatments, because of the employer's application of its absence-management policies.

The right to request flexible working

The right to request flexible working offers a potential framework that could enable those undergoing ART treatments to combine treatment while remaining in work. This right extends to all employees with 26 weeks continuity of employment.[16] Previously this was limited to persons with caring responsibilities but is no longer restricted to certain groups, now extending to all employees.[17] This enables an employee to request a change in his or her hours, time and/or place of work.[18] Changes made are permanent, although the statute requires that employees 'specify the changes applied for' when making their application, which would appear to allow, or at least not prevent, changes of limited duration being applied for in the original request.[19] This could be useful for those undergoing ART treatments as it would, in principle, enable them to modify their working arrangements to allow them to undergo a course of treatment.

However, this right is only a right to request flexible working and not a right to change working patterns and is consequently a weak right in practice.[20] The burdens on employees making the request are high. They must specify that it is such a request, indicate the changes sought and when they would come into effect and identify the effect it would have on the employer and how that could be dealt with.[21] The employer, in contrast, has only an obligation to 'deal with the application in a reasonable manner'

15 See further: Astra Emir, *Selwyn's Law of Employment* (20th edn, OUP 2018) paras.17.103–17.113.
16 Flexible Working Regulations 2014, SI2014/1398, Reg.3.
17 Children and Families Act 2014, s.131.
18 ERA, s.80F(1).
19 *Ibid*, s.80F(2)(b).
20 Grace James, 'The Work and Families Act 2006: Legislation to Improve Choice and Flexibility?' [2006] 35(3) ILJ 272, 277.
21 ERA, s.80F(2).

and to inform employees of their decision.²² There are no requirements for
the decision to be reasonable and no recourse to challenge the reasonable-
ness of the decision itself.²³ However, when first enacted, Anderson suggested that the requirement to put the reasons for refusal in writing could
be useful for employees pursuing claims on other grounds, for example
discrimination.²⁴ Nevertheless, the employer can justify its refusal of the
request on numerous grounds,²⁵ making it easy for the employer to deny
requests in practice. If the employer does refuse, the employee will have to
wait another year before making a new request as only one can be made in
a one-year period.²⁶

While requesting a change in working arrangement may be beneficial
for those undergoing ART treatments during the treatment process, this is
unlikely to require a permanent change in working arrangements. Even if
an employer were to accept a temporary change in working arrangements,
given the unpredictability of success rates for treatment, this may be insufficient. In addition, given the specificity required in making such a request
in the first instance,²⁷ the changes made may not be sufficiently flexible to
respond to the, at times, unpredictable requirements of treatment. Furthermore, the lack of guarantees that requests will be granted as well as the
acceptable timeframes in which decisions should be made²⁸ means that this
right in practice offers little support for those undergoing ART treatments
to re-arrange their work to accommodate treatment.

Rights to time off during the ante-natal period

There are several rights to time off during the ante-natal or pre-placement
for adoption period that could be extended to include those undergoing
ART treatments. These include the right to paid time off for ante-natal care
for the pregnant employee;²⁹ the unpaid right of a partner of a pregnant
woman and of commissioning parents in surrogacy situations, to accompany

22 *Ibid*, s.80G(4)(1)(a)–(aa).
23 *Ibid*, s.80H. Grace James, 'Mothers and Fathers as Parents and Workers; Family
    Friendly Employment Policies in an Era of Shifting Identities' [2009] 31(3) JSWFL
    271, 278.
24 Lucy Anderson, 'Sound Bite Legislation: The Employment Act 2002 and New Flex-
    ible Working "Rights" for Parents' [2003] 32(1) ILJ 37, 41.
25 ERA, s.80G(4)(1)(b).
26 *Ibid*, s.80F(4).
27 *Hussain v Consumer Credit Counselling*, ET Case No.1804305/04.
28 Within three months or longer if both agree: ERA, s.80G(1B).
29 *Ibid*, ss.55–57.

the pregnant woman when attending two ante-natal appointments;[30] and the rights of adopting parents to attend either five paid or two unpaid pre-placement meetings.[31] While there are various limitations to these rights themselves, particularly given the limited number of appointments and lack of paid leave for 'secondary' parents,[32] some lessons can be learned for those undergoing ART treatments. Also notable is that employees utilising these rights are protected by the right not to suffer a detriment and protection against dismissal if the reason, or principal reason, is because they exercised any of these rights.[33] This ensures that not only can they access these rights but that they are also protected while doing so. Any rights extended to those undergoing ART treatments should also include these protections. The potential of these rights, and the underpinning legal frameworks, to extend to those undergoing ART treatments and their partners are considered in turn.

An analogous right to time off work to undergo ART treatments could be created mirroring the framework of the right to paid time off work to attend ante-natal appointments. This right is not limited by any continuity of employment requirements, nor is it limited to a specific length of time per appointment. The only limitations are that the employee is pregnant and that she has been advised to attend such appointments by a medical practitioner, registered midwife or registered nurse.[34] Other than for the first appointment, the employer can request evidence of the employee's pregnancy and of appointments scheduled.[35] A similar right for those undergoing ART treatments would recognise that such employees require comparable access to medical appointments and/or treatment and a corresponding right to paid time off to facilitate this. Such a right could be framed in the same way as the right to ante-natal care, with employers having the right to request evidence of undergoing treatment and of appointments scheduled in the same way, as well as having not being able to refuse access to such treatment. Such a right offers the ideal response to the current gap in the legal framework, because it would signify that this experience is valued and would facilitate its normalisation. While recent research undertaken by Payne et al. shows that most people undergoing treatment do disclose this to their employer in order to gain time off

---

30 *Ibid*, ss.57ZE–57ZF.
31 *Ibid*, ss.57ZE(7)(e)–(f).
32 Michelle Weldon-Johns, 'From Modern Workplaces to Modern Families – Re-envisioning the Work – Family Conflict' [2015] 37(4) JSWFL 395, 405–6.
33 ERA, s.47C and s.99.
34 *Ibid*, s.55(1).
35 *Ibid*, ss.55(2)–(3).

work, many would still prefer not to. The reasons given include privacy; not understanding; negative career impact, including the tensions between work and undergoing treatment; stigma; negative attitudes; confidences being breached; and not wanting special treatment.[36] The lack of a legal framework and consequent diversity in employer's responses was also a factor.[37] While this research indicates that specific employment rights would be beneficial here, it also underscores that this may be challenging for those who do not want to disclose, particularly in the absence of overarching equality law protections. Consequently, a similar framework could be used to underpin an equivalent general right to leave for those undergoing treatment, discussed later.

A similar right for a partner to take time off to accompany a woman undergoing ART treatments to that available to partners of pregnant women would also be beneficial here. However, the right to unpaid time off to accompany a pregnant woman to two ante-natal appointments of a maximum of 6.5 hours each is insufficient for pregnancy,[38] let alone for those undergoing ART treatments. A more useful framework is that provided for adoptive parents, where one parent is entitled to attend five paid pre-placement meetings,[39] although the other is only entitled to unpaid time off to attend two such appointments.[40] Focusing on the former right, the employee is entitled to attend these appointments subject to providing the employer with evidence, if requested, of the appointment and that the employee has elected to exercise this right where he or she is one of two joint adopters.[41] While these are also limited to 6.5 hours off per appointment,[42] they otherwise provide enhanced rights in comparison with partners and commissioning parents. While this is an attempt to mirror the framework for pregnant employees, it nevertheless fails to adequately reflect the position of alternative family forms.[43] However, it does offer a useful starting point for developing a framework for the partners of those undergoing ART treatments. While it also may be unnecessary for the partner to accompany the woman to all appointments, a more broadly defined right to attend a greater number of appointments, particularly those during which treatment will be carried out, would be welcome. The position of

---

36 Payne, Seenan and van den Akker (n.5), 160–63.
37 *Ibid*, 156–57, 159.
38 ERA, ss.57ZE(2)–(3); Weldon-Johns (n.32), 405–6.
39 *Ibid*, ss.57ZJ(4)–(5) and s.57ZK.
40 *Ibid*, s.57ZL.
41 *Ibid*, ss.57ZJ(8)–(9).
42 *Ibid*, s.57ZJ(6).
43 Weldon-Johns (n.32), 405–6.

commissioning parents in surrogacy should not be forgotten here. While certain rights have been extended to them, as discussed in Chapter 2, these focus on the post-conception period and similarly ignore their experiences in their journey to parenthood, which begin much earlier and may also involve them personally undergoing ART treatments. Consequently, the rights proposed here would similarly extend to them, including enabling them to attend ART appointments with the surrogate. While it would also be preferable to frame this as a right to accompany someone undergoing ART treatments, similar concerns raised earlier are equally applicable here. Nevertheless, this framework also offers a useful starting point for proposing an equivalent right to accompany someone undergoing treatment, as discussed later.

This discussion of current UK work-family rights underscores not only the limitations of the existing frameworks but also the potential for rights to be extended to those undergoing ART treatments, their partners and commissioning parents. This discussion has also highlighted the potential challenges of opting for specific rights for those undergoing ART treatments with requirements of disclosure, particularly without an overarching equality law framework extending protection to them throughout the treatment process. The following section examines the possibility of a more general right to medical leave to address this gap, with reference to the experience in the US.

A right to medical leave

An alternative to a specific rights approach is instead enacting a more general right to medical leave. This could address some of the concerns regarding disclosure and could be related to the rights already available under the SSP framework. However, proposing a right to medical leave is also problematic because it returns to the comparison and assimilation with sickness, which pregnancy discrimination has strived to move away from. However, unlike pregnancy, those undergoing ART treatments are engaged in medical treatments and procedures. In these respects, the need to accommodate time off to undergo treatment and attend appointments can be conceptualised as a right to time off for medical leave. The experience of the US is again relevant here, and the rights to leave contained within the FMLA are considered next to assess what lessons can be learned from them.

The FMLA

The FMLA contains gender-neutral rights to leave for either family or medical purposes. The right does not automatically include those undergoing

ART treatments, although its potential to do so is considered later. The rights are only available to those employees who satisfy certain fairly restrictive conditions. In the first instance, employees must have 12 months' continuous service with their current employer and have worked a minimum of 1,250 hours in the previous 12 months period.[44] This requirement restricts the rights to US citizens, with an established labour market attachment and those who work full-time or long part-time hours. Such a requirement excludes many employees, particularly those in atypical or part-time work. There are also specific exceptions to these provisions for certain federal officers or employees and employers engaging fewer than 50 employees at a particular worksite and within a 75-mile radius.[45] Consequently, many employees fall outside of the scope of the act in practice. There are also certain restrictions that may prevent employees from using leave. While employees have the right to return to work in their previous or an equivalent position if they do so before or at the end of the maximum leave period,[46] there is a specific exception for those within the highest-paid 10% of the company.[47] This exception applies when the return of such an employee would result in severe economic loss to the employer.[48] This may further reduce the number of employees who request leave in practice.

For those who do qualify, they are entitled to a total of 12 normal workweeks of unpaid leave, for either family or medical purposes, during any 12-month period.[49] There are three categories of rights they can utilise: two rights to family care leave, the right to medical leave and a right relating to having a family member in the armed forces.[50] The family care situations encompass two distinct circumstances: the care of children on entering the family, and the care of family members who are ill. For present purposes, the most relevant is the right to medical leave, which can be used because of a serious health condition which prevents them from working.[51]

For those undergoing ART treatments in the US, the question of whether they would be entitled to leave under the FMLA turns on whether this is a serious health condition. This is defined as 'illnesses, injuries, impairments, or physical or mental conditions which involve inpatient care' or

---

44 FMLA, §101(2)(A).
45 *Ibid*, §101(2)(B).
46 *Ibid*, §104(a)(1). Further defined: 29 CFR 825 (Code of Federal Regulations, The Family and Medical Leave Act), (29 CFR 825) §825.214–§825.215.
47 *Ibid*, §104(b)(2). Further defined in: 29 CFR 825, §825.217.
48 *Ibid*, §104(b)(1). Further defined in: 29 CFR 825, §825.218.
49 *Ibid*, §§102(a)(1) and (c).
50 *Ibid*, §102(a)(1).
51 *Ibid*, §102(a)(1)(D).

'continuing treatment by a health care provider.'[52] *Continuing treatment* is further defined as a period of incapacity of more than three consecutive days and any related treatment or period of incapacity that also includes two or more treatments within 30 days of the first day of incapacity or at least one treatment with related course of treatment under the supervision of the health care provider.[53] Infertility and/or undergoing ART treatment can relate to a physical impairment or condition that, at times, requires inpatient care and/or continuing treatment. This will often include two or more treatments within a 30-day period and/or a course of treatment following an initial procedure. Given that infertility has been recognised within the scope of the ADA, it is likely that it would fall within the definition of serious health condition here too.[54] However, the requirement for more than three consecutive days incapacity in the first instance and whether all related appointments and the impact of treatment are included is unclear.

This issue was considered, in part, by the 6th Circuit COA in *Culpepper v BlueCross BlueShield of Tennessee Inc.*[55] In this case, the plaintiff had 13 days of unexcused absence on her record that was contrary to her employer's Incident Report Policy, which permitted dismissal after more than 5 such absences. Culpepper argued that 11 of these were related to undergoing ART treatments and had medical evidence that supported two separate periods of three-day absences relating to treatment, which the employer accepted were covered by the FMLA. Notably, the previous District Court observed that the act requires more than three days' absence in order to amount to a serious health condition but did not consider this further as the employer had waived its right to challenge it by granting leave.[56] The COA upheld the District Court decision to grant summary judgement to the employer because there was insufficient medical evidence to support her claim that she was incapable of working, per the requirements of the FMLA, during the other absences.[57] This decision underscores the difficulty of each period of absence meeting the requisite standard of incapability and importance of unequivocal medical evidence to support every absence, even when parts of the period may be included within the scope of

---

52 *Ibid*, §101(11). Further defined: 29 CFR 825, §825.113–§825.115.

53 29 CFR 825, §825.102 and §825.115.

54 Kerry Van der Burch, 'Courts' Struggle with Infertility: The Impact of *Hall v. Nalco* on Infertility-Related Employment Discrimination' [2010] 81 University of Colorado L Rev 545, 575–77.

55 No. 08–5204.

56 *Culpepper v BlueCross BlueShield of Tennessee Inc* No. 1:07-CV-48, fn1.

57 *Culpepper* (n.55), 9–11.

the FMLA. While this appears to suggest that undergoing ART treatments can fall within the scope of the FMLA, given that it was not contested here, it is questionable whether anything can be learned from the decision with respect to the rights of those undergoing ART treatments.

While the decision does not directly endorse the employer's decision to accept undergoing IVF treatment within the scope of the FMLA, there are two possible readings of it. Optimistically, the decision can be viewed as supporting the possibility that undergoing ART treatments is within the scope of serious health conditions if sufficient medical evidence is produced to support incapability for work while undergoing treatment. This was the case here with respect to the excused periods. Medical evidence was provided by her doctor, who classified undergoing IVF treatment as a serious health condition for the purposes of the FMLA.[58] More realistically, it reinforces the challenges of satisfying this definition in practice. The treatment, and/or its effects, must last at for at least four consecutive days for the FMLA to apply. Thus, meaning that initial investigations, one-off procedures and treatments are unlikely to satisfy this definition. This mirrors the problem in the UK context regarding the availability of SSP. On balance, it probably reflects a mid-point of view. Some treatments will fall within the scope of the FMLA, but not all,[59] again mirroring the patchwork of rights available in the UK context. With that in mind, what lessons can be learned from the US experience?

There are several other aspects of the US experience that can be drawn from in developing an equivalent right in the UK. For instance, the right to medical leave can be taken on an intermittent basis or on a reduced leave schedule, where is it deemed medically necessary.[60] This enables qualifying employees to either take separate periods of leave relating to the same condition or to reduce their working schedule, usually in terms of days or hours, for a specific period.[61] There has to be a medical reason as to why leave should be taken in this way,[62] and employees must make reasonable efforts to ensure that any treatment scheduled does not unduly interfere with the employer's operations.[63] The overall maximum duration of leave remains 12 normal workweeks, so employees do not lose any entitlements by using leave in this way.[64] If those undergoing ART treatments were

---

58 *Culpepper* (n.55), 2–3.
59 Cushing (n.3), 1725–26.
60 FMLA, §102(b)(1).
61 29 CFR 825, §825.202.
62 *Ibid.*
63 *Ibid*, §825.203.
64 FMLA, §102(b)(1).

accepted within the scope of the legislation, this flexibility would be beneficial because often treatments require numerous appointments and absences over a concentrated, but not necessarily continuous, period. Given that the required flexibility would be directly related to undergoing treatment, it is likely to be considered medically necessary by their health care provider and so should meet the qualifying criteria here. This reinforces the importance of the possibility of flexible working arrangements that genuinely enable employees to combine work with other life commitments.

The availability of flexibility in notification requirements would also be beneficial for those undergoing ART treatments. Under the FMLA if the requirement for leave is foreseeable, employees must make reasonable efforts to schedule treatment in such in a way that it does not unduly interfere with the employer's operations and provide the employer with at least 30 days' notice or as soon as is practicable if treatment must begin sooner, of their intention to undergo treatment.[65] For those undergoing ART treatments, it may be challenging to meet the 30-day requirement because of the sometimes unpredictable and time-sensitive requirements for treatment. While notice should then be given as soon as is practicable, this could result in employees taking leave before they know if it is covered by the act, leaving them vulnerable to disciplinary action if it is not.[66] While a degree of flexibility is beneficial here, it is most effective when it enables individuals to exercise rights in practice. Consequently, an expediated decision-making process in those instances would also be useful.

The US experience also highlights that the most limited aspect of this right is the absence of a requirement for paid leave.[67] It is possible for an employer to provide paid leave or for an employee to decide, or an employer to require, that the leave be substituted with accrued leave which has a paid element.[68] However, this often means foregoing another right to paid leave, and many workers will only be entitled to unpaid leave. This reinforces the importance of creating a stand-alone right to paid leave in the UK context, and/or linking this with existing rights to SSP.

While the right to medical leave in the US has many shortcomings and may not actually include those undergoing ART treatments within its scope, it nevertheless provides a useful framework for developing a similar right in the UK. It reinforces the importance of creating a right to leave, which clearly includes those undergoing ART treatments within its scope.

---

65 *Ibid*, §102(e)(2).
66 As seen in *Culpepper* (n.55).
67 FMLA, §102(c).
68 *Ibid*, §§102(d). See further: 29 CFR 825, §825.207.

The qualifying criteria should also not be so onerous as to exclude most employees from its scope. There should be flexibility in the notice requirements, and in how the rights can be utilised in practice. It also should be a right to paid leave, and there should be sufficient employment protection provisions both during leave and on returning to work to not only encourage people to use leave time but also protect them while doing so.

A right to time off work to undergo ART treatments: possibilities for the UK

The foregoing has shown the importance of creating a clear right to leave that will enable those undergoing ART treatments to take paid time off work to do so while also ensuring their privacy regarding undergoing treatment. A right to medical leave offers the most suitable solution here. The experiences of the US coupled with the existing frameworks in the UK indicate that a general right to medical leave can offer some potential here. This right could be expressed as a right to time off work to attend medical appointments and/or undergo treatment relating to a serious health condition. Such treatment may include investigatory appointments and/or procedures and outpatient and/or inpatient treatments. This would mirror the US framework to some extent. It is acknowledged that the reference to a 'serious health condition' could be problematic, because adopting a narrow interpretation here could exclude those undergoing ART treatments. However, in *Culpepper*, the exclusion of absences from the FMLA was largely related to the requirement for a minimum of more than three consecutive days incapacity, rather than the seriousness of the health condition itself.[69] Furthermore, it is likely to be preferable, from a policy point of view, to limit those entitled to this right so that it does not include all routine appointments with health care providers. Consequently, the requirement for treatment to be related to a serious health condition would ensure that it was not overbroad, and other steps could be taken to ensure those undergoing ART treatments are included. This could be achieved by including those undergoing ART treatments, for whatever reason, within the scope of the definition of serious health conditions in the legislation.

Given that the rights to attend and accompany those attending antenatal appointments contain no continuity of employment requirements, the right to medical leave should similarly be a day-one right. This would ensure that all employees are entitled to time off for such purposes. Qualifying conditions should relate solely to the production of relevant medical

69 However, this was not directly examined.

evidence of the dates and times of appointments and/or treatments, as well as confirmation by the medical practitioner that they are related to a serious health condition, as defined in the legislation. This could be framed in such a way that the specific health condition does not need to be identified, to ensure that employee's desire not to disclose would not be compromised but would still require confirmation of such a condition by a prescribed medical practitioner.

The right should be framed as a right to paid leave. While it would be preferable to also frame this as a day-one right, other rights to leave in the UK separate the entitlement to leave from that to pay. A similar approach would be consistent with that. As a minimum, this could replicate the right to SSP and its qualifying conditions regarding pay. This would ensure consistency and would also enhance those rights by ensuring that individuals requiring time off to undergo medical treatment and/or attend medical appointments have the right to time off work in order to do so. However, if it were to be intrinsically linked to the right to SSP, then individuals would not be covered for one-off appointments, at least under the current legal framework. Given that the requirement for minimum days of incapacity in the first instance has been a potential barrier in the US context, this requirement should not be replicated in UK legislation. Instead, this could be amended to allow payments to be made to those undergoing such treatment, with these periods being deducted from the overall SSP benefit entitlement.

If the right is framed as a specific right to medical leave that can be used in any given 12-month period, then it should be long enough to facilitate undergoing a course of treatment, and flexible enough to recognise that not all courses of treatment are continuous and require consecutive periods of absence. The right to 12 weeks' medical leave in the US offers a useful comparison here. It is longer than the 28-week benefit entitlement to SSP, which extends over three years, but is, in any event, distinguishable from it because that applies more generally to incapacity for work and not just attending medical appointments and/or undergoing treatment. This again underscores that while there is a potential connection between these rights, there are clear distinctions between the purposes of both. However, the right to medical leave could be mapped onto SSP if the overall period was extended. This could reduce the potential burdens on business in implementing this right in practice.

The possibility for flexibility in the utilisation of the leave, as is possible in the US, would also be beneficial here. This could facilitate a range of flexible working options including continuous periods of absence, single days, partial days and reduced daily working hours. Specifying the right in terms of days' leave or hours could further support this as opposed to focusing on weekly periods, the problems with which were evident in the context of the right to unpaid parental leave.[70] While this flexibility is unlikely to be welcomed by employers, a requirement that the medical practitioner treating the employee recommend and/or support the employees' use of leave in this way to facilitate treatment should prevent misuse in practice. Framing the right in this way would help address some of the inflexibility concerns raised earlier with using the right to request flexible working to accommodate treatment while enabling employees to create flexibility on a temporary basis.

Alongside the right to time off work to attend medical appointments, there should also be a day-one right to paid time off work to accompany someone attending such appointments. This would again be akin to the existing framework relating to ante-natal and adoption placement meetings and could be limited to a certain number or certain kind of appointments, such as when they are undergoing significant forms of treatment, where additional care and/or support may be beneficial and/or required. Again, employers could request a declaration of the appointment information and that the employee is in a recognised relationship with the person undergoing treatment in the same way as is currently required for those attending ante-natal appointments.

To strengthen these rights, they should be accompanied with both the right not to suffer a detriment and the right to protection against dismissal for utilising, proposing to use or having exercised them. The framework for such protections is also present in the ERA in relation to other rights to time off work and could again be mirrored here. This is even more important if the overarching equality law framework has not been extended to include those undergoing ART treatments.

The foregoing shows that a right to leave that would enable those undergoing ART treatments to take time off work to attend such appointments and/or undergo treatments is both conceptually and practically consistent with the current UK legal framework. Whether this is expressed as a specific right to time off to undergo ART treatments, or a more general right to medical leave, the existing rights around pregnancy and the pre-natal period, as well as the right to SSP, offer useful starting points to extend rights in a meaningful way. Drawing from the lessons of the US experience, a flexible, paid, day-one right to leave that includes employment protection and that extends not only to those undergoing treatment but also in some instances their partners and commissioning parents would ensure that those engaged in treatment can do so without having the additional burden of job insecurity. This is all the more important if a reinterpretation of the boundaries of the equality law frameworks cannot be achieved but remains so even if they are.

Conclusion

The right to time off work to undergo ART treatments is integral to the development of a legal framework that both recognises and values the experiences of those engaged in them. While a specific right aimed solely at those undergoing treatment is preferable, the realities of the difficulties in exercising such a right in practice are acknowledged. These challenges are particularly marked in the absence of an overarching equality law framework that affords protection to those undergoing ART treatments. Consequently, the more general right to medical leave presented here offers a more meaningful solution in the meantime. Drawing from the experience in the US, this analysis has shown that it is possible to expand the current UK work-family rights framework to include such a right. This could easily mirror the other rights that enable employees to take time off work for reasons relating to care and/or impending parenthood. The extension of these rights to either specifically those undergoing ART treatments or in the form of a more general, but still focused, right to medical leave would be both practically and conceptually consistent with the existing frameworks. This would be an important step forward in ensuring that those undergoing ART treatments are both recognised and protected within the UK legal framework, as they attempt to combine treatment while retaining their labour market position. Indeed, it may be the first step necessary for facilitating the broader reinterpretation of the boundaries of equality law.

6 Conclusions

Introduction

The purpose of this book has been to expose the gaps within the UK employment and equality law frameworks for those undergoing ART treatments. In doing so, the vulnerable position of those undergoing treatment without recourse to an underpinning legal framework has been highlighted, as has the stark gap between the framework regulating treatment and that protecting the lived experiences of those trying to achieve a family while remaining in work. The aims of this book have been to, firstly, re-examine the UK equality law framework to determine if it can be reinterpreted to include those undergoing ART treatments and, secondly, examine whether a specific right to time off work to undergo treatment can be included within the employment law framework. The examination undertaken in this book has shown that not only is this possible but also is long overdue, particularly in comparison with the US. In doing so, the following issues emerge as key considerations that must be acknowledged in future attempts to embrace the experiences of those undergoing ART treatments within the legal frameworks.

Recognising alternative routes to parenthood

The examination in this book has reinforced that despite the highly regulated legal framework surrounding both the provision of ART treatments and parental status, discussed in Chapter 1, alternative routes to parenthood are not fully embraced within the equality and employment law frameworks. This exclusion from these legal frameworks is inconsistent with their wider acceptance within the family law sphere. As the jurisdictions within the UK are examining the legal framework on surrogacy,[1] now is the time

---

1 Law Commission, *Thirteenth Programme of Law Reform* (Law Com No.377, 2017) 2.40–2.44; Scottish Law Commission, *Tenth Programme of Law Reform* (Law Com No.250, 2018) 2.32–2.37.

to also examine the interrelationships between these areas of law. In particular, to consider how those engaged in alternative routes to parenthood are supported and protected while doing so. The re-examination of the protected characteristics in Chapters 3 and 4 demonstrate that they can be interpreted more broadly to include these alternative routes to parenthood within their scope. The examination of the gaps within the work-family rights legislation in Chapter 5 also demonstrates that the UK is well-placed to develop the existing framework to include alternative routes to parenthood. This could easily be achieved by mirroring the existing rights in the pre-natal period and adapting them to reflect the lived experiences of those engaged in ART treatments and the impact of this on their working lives.

Recognising the social value of procreation

The social value of procreation and the inherently gendered experience of childbearing have been referred to in several decisions discussed throughout the book. The importance of recognising its value has often been a central consideration in extending protection to those undergoing ART treatments, as is evident in the discussion of the US jurisprudence in Chapters 3 and 4. Nevertheless, it is also apparent that both remain undervalued and under-protected within the EU and UK legal frameworks. Only by recognising their value, and by protecting women in all those instances when they are engaged in this, can equality law truly protect women from all the burdens of combining childbearing and professional life. The intersectionality analysis undertaken in this book facilitates this from the perspectives of both disability intersecting with gender, recognising women's experiences of disability, and gender intersecting with disability, recognising women's childbearing capacity and the need to accommodate this. However, it is important to draw clear distinctions between childbearing, which is sex-specific, and childcare, which is gender-neutral. Failing to do so will continue to reinforce undesirable ideologies of motherhood which undermine gender equality and fathers' childcaring roles.

Overcoming barriers

Another central consideration is the requirement to overcome a range of barriers which exclude those engaged in ART treatments from legal rights and protections. Many of these disabling barriers are created by the limitations within the legislation itself; however, there are also wider societal barriers to be overcome. Those identified within the book include concerns about the tensions between combining undergoing treatment and work; the impact of treatment on professional life; stigma around undergoing treatment, infertility and involuntary childlessness; failing to recognise the value of procreation and its impact on women's professional lives; and, of course, the lack of a legal framework. All these barriers can be overcome by recognising the experiences of those engaged in treatment within the legal frameworks in the ways proposed in the book.

Adopting an intersectional analysis

The analysis undertaken in this book reinforces that multidimensional or intersectional discrimination must be embedded in the future development of equality law. Schiek's intersecting nodes approach has provided a useful analytical and interpretative model that can facilitate such an analysis in this context.[2] The examinations in Chapters 3 and 4 reinforce that it is only by analysing these experiences through the intersecting lenses of gender and disability that the disadvantages faced can be brought into focus, enabling protection to be afforded. From a disability perspective, this ensures that women's experiences of disability are valued, as opposed to being rendered invisible. It also recognises that reproduction is a central life activity, thus recognising the social value of procreation. This is also acknowledged from a pregnancy-related perspective, as is its impact on women's working lives. It also recognises the inherently gendered experiences of childbearing, which extend to those pursuing pregnancy through ART treatments and the need to accommodate these differences to achieve gender equality. In doing so, alternative routes to parenthood are recognised and valued. This reinforces that the future direction of equality and employment law must recognise and embed intersectionality in the framing of disputes and the interpretation of the boundaries of the legislation in practice.

Recommendations

The alternative conceptualisations of equality law and extension of employment rights presented here cannot be achieved on their own. However, small but significant changes can be made to facilitate this. Multidimensional, if not yet intersectional, discrimination can be embraced by simply bringing s.14 of the EqA into force. This would allow claims to be presented on dual grounds, with reference to the protected characteristics contained in the act. While limited to dual grounds, it would enable those engaged

---

2 Dagmar Schiek, 'Organizing EU Equality Law Around the Nodes of "Race", Gender and Disability' in Dagmar Schiek and Anna Lawson (eds), *European Union Non-discrimination Law and Intersectionality: Investigating the Triangle of Racial, Gender and Disability Discrimination* (Ashgate Publishing 2011).

in ART treatments to articulate their claims through the dual lenses of dis-ability and gender. It would then be open to the courts to examine these experiences in an intersectional way, as envisaged in Chapters 3 and 4. In addition, in the context of disability intersecting with gender, this would be consistent with the recommendations of the Committee on the Rights of Persons with Disabilities and the UK's obligations under the CRPD.[3]

Other minor amendments could be made to s.18 EqA to include under-going ART treatments as a pregnancy-related condition. This would require changing the reference to 'illness suffered by her as a result of' pregnancy, to pregnancy-related conditions and removing the limitation, in this regard, to pre-existing pregnancy. This would enable the asymmetri-cal approach afforded to pregnancy to be extended to those engaged in ART treatments, reflecting the analogous justifications for protection in both instances. Furthermore, the EHRC guidance could be updated to reflect these reinterpretations of equality law. In particular, the guidance could be revised to clarify the instances when discrimination by associa-tion with a pregnant woman would give rise to a sex discrimination claim.[4] This should specifically include commissioning parents in surrogacy. The guidance on IVF treatments should also be revised:[5] firstly, to reflect the broader range of ART treatments available and, secondly, to embrace the intersectional analysis adopted in Chapters 3 and 4. This would include recognising that less favourable treatment could amount to disability dis-crimination, reflecting the gendered experiences of infertility as a disability. It would also include recognising that undergoing ART treatments is either pregnancy-related or based on childbearing capacity, and so less favourable treatment relating to this is direct sex discrimination.

Finally, specific rights to time off work should be extended both to those engaged in treatment and their partners. This should reflect existing rights afforded in the pre-natal period within the ERA[6] and either be framed as specific rights for those engaged in ART treatments or as a more general right to medical leave, reflecting the challenges and barriers to disclosure experienced by some of those engaged in treatment. These recommen-dations underscore that extending these rights and protections to those engaged in ART treatments in the UK is not only conceptually consistent

3 Committee on the Rights of Persons with Disabilities, *Concluding Observations on the Initial Report of the United Kingdom of Great Britain and Northern Ireland* (CRPD/C/GBR/CO/1, 2017) [15], [19].
4 Equality and Human Rights Commission (EHRC), *Equality Act 2010: Employment Statutory Code of Practice* (EHRC 2011) 3.18.
5 *Ibid*, 8.44, 17.28–17.29.
6 Ss.55–57ZS.

with the existing legal framework but is also achievable in practice if parliament is minded to do so.

Conclusion

For too long, the burdens and risks of undergoing ART treatments, including those relating to employment security, have fallen solely on the shoulders of these working women. Now is the time to conceive a new interpretation of equality law that recognises alternative routes to parenthood and the need to accommodate them in the employment sphere. Extending rights and protections to those engaged in ART treatments ensures that their experiences are acknowledged and normalised within the legal framework, which can also help reduce the continuing stigma experienced by some of those engaged in treatment. As the UK looks ahead, not only with its revisions to surrogacy law but also towards an unknown future in the context of employment and equality law, it should do so in way that is progressive, embraces new routes to parenthood, breaks down barriers and genuinely values childbearing and its impact on women's labour market engagement. In doing so, it can lead the way forward in recognising the rights of those engaged in ART treatments.

Bibliography

'2000/750/EC: Council Decision of 27 November 2000 Establishing a Community Action Programme to Combat Discrimination (2001 to 2006)' [2000] OJL 303, 2 December 2000.

ACAS (Advice, Conciliation and Arbitration Service), 'Employees' Rights during IVF Treatment' <www.acas.org.uk/index.aspx?articleid=5457> accessed 30 July 2019.

Anderson, Lucy, 'Sound Bite Legislation: The Employment Act 2002 and New Flexible Working 'Rights' for Parents' [2003] 32(1) ILJ 37.

Atkinson, Jamie, 'Shared Parental Leave in the UK: Can It Advance Gender Equality by Changing Fathers into Co-parents?' [2017] 13(3) Int JLC 356.

Batavia Andrew I, and Kay Schriner, 'The Americans With Disabilities Act as Engine of Social Change: Models of Disability and the Potential of a Civil Rights Approach' [2001] 29(4) Policy Studies Journal 690.

Beecroft, Adrian, *Report on Employment Law* (URN 12/825 2011).

Begum, Nasa, 'Disabled Women and the Feminist Agenda' [1992] 40 Feminist Review 70.

Bell, Mark, 'The Principle of Equal Treatment: Widening and Deepening' in Paul Craig and Gráinne De Búrca (eds), *The Evolution of EU Law* (OUP 2011).

Bentley, Cintra D, 'A Pregnant Pause: Are Women Who Undergo Fertility Treatment to Achieve Pregnancy within the Scope of Title VII's Pregnancy Discrimination Act' [1998] 73 Chi-Kent L Rev 391.

Bullock, Jess and Annick Masselot, 'Multiple Discrimination and Intersectional Disadvantages: Challenges and Opportunities in the European Union Legal Framework' [2012–2013] 19 Colum J Eur L 57.

Burri, Susanne, 'Care in Family Relations: The Case of Surrogacy Leave' [2015] 17(2) EJLR 271.

Busby, Nicole and Michelle Weldon-Johns, 'Fathers as Carers in UK Law and Policy: Dominant Ideologies and Lived Experience' [2019] 41(3) JSWFL 280.

Butlin, Sarah Fraser, 'The UN Convention on the Rights of Persons with Disabilities: Does the Equality Act 2010 Measure up to UK International Commitments?' [2011] 40(4) ILJ 428.

Chege, Victoria, 'The European Union Anti-discrimination Directives and European Union Equality Law: The Case of Multidimensional Discrimination' [2012] 13(2) ERA Forum 275.

Committee on the Rights of Persons with Disabilities, *Concluding Observations on the Initial Report of the United Kingdom of Great Britain and Northern Ireland* (CRPD/C/GBR/CO/1, 2017).

Conaghan, Joanne, 'Intersectionality and the Feminist Project in Law' in Emily Grabham, Davina Cooper, Jane Krishnadas and Didi Herman (eds) *Intersectionality and Beyond: Law, Power and the Politics of Location* (Routledge Cavendish 2009).

Cousins, Mel, 'Surrogacy Leave and EU Law. Case C-167/12 CD v ST and Case C-363/12 Z v A Government Department' [2014] 21(3) MJ 476.

Crenshaw, Kimberle, 'Demarginalizing the Intersection of Race and Sex: A Black Feminist Critique of Antidiscrimination Doctrine, Feminist Theory and Antiracist Politics' [1989] 1(Article 8) U Chi Legal F 137.

Cushing, Katie, 'Facing Reality: The Pregnancy Discrimination Act Falls Short for Women Undergoing Infertility Treatment' [2010] 40 Seton Hall L Rev 1697.

Dallmann, Deborah K, 'The Lay View of What "Disability" Means Must Give Way to What Congress Says It Means: Infertility as a "Disability" Under the Americans with Disabilities Act' [1996] 38(1) Wm & Mary L Rev 371.

Deardorff, Michelle D, 'Beyond Pregnancy: Litigating Infertility, Contraception, and Breastfeeding in the Workplace' [2011] 32(1) Journal of Women, Politics & Policy 52.

De Baere, Geert, 'Shall I be Mother? The Prohibition on Sex Discrimination, the UN Disability Convention, and the Right to Surrogacy Leave under EU Law' [2015] CLJ 44.

Deech, Ruth and Anna Smajdor, *From IVF to Immortality: Controversy in the Era of Reproductive Technology* (OUP 2007).

Degener, Theresia 'The Definition of Disability in German and Foreign Discrimination Law' [2006] 26(2) Disability Studies Quarterly.

Degener, Theresia, 'Disability in a Human Rights Context' [2016] 5(3) Laws 35.

Dickens, Linda, 'The Road Is Long: Thirty Years of Equality Legislation in Britain' [2007] 45(3) British Journal of Industrial Relations 463.

Di Torella, Eugenia Caracciolo, 'Brave New Fathers for a Brave New World? Fathers as Caregivers in an Evolving European Union' [2014] 20(1) Eur LJ 88.

Di Torella, Eugenia Caracciolo, 'Men in the Work/Family Reconciliation Discourse: The Swallows That Did Not Make a Summer?' [2015] 37(3) JSWFL 334.

Di Torella, Eugenia Caracciolo and Petra Foubert, 'Surrogacy, Pregnancy and Maternity Rights: A Missed Opportunity for a More Coherent Regime of Parental Rights in the EU' [2015] EL Rev 52.

Di Torella, Eugenia Caracciolo and Annick Masselot, 'Pregnancy, Maternity and the Organisation of Family Life: An Attempt to Classify the Case Law of the Court of Justice' [2001] 26(3) EL Rev 239.

Doyle, Brian, 'Employment Rights, Equal Opportunities and Disabled Persons: The Ingredients for Reform' [1993] 22(2) IJL 89.

Emir, Astra, *Selwyn's Law of Employment* (20th edn, OUP 2018).

Equality and Human Rights Commission, *Equality Act 2010: Employment Statutory Code of Practice* (EHRC, 2011).

Esping-Andersen, Gosta, *Social Foundations of Postindustrial Economies* (OUP 1999).

Ewing, Kate, 'Surrogacy: Beyond Equality?' [2014] 120(April) Emp LB 6.

Favalli Silvia and Delia Ferri, 'Tracing the Boundaries between Disability and Sickness in the European Union: Squaring the Circle?' [2016] 23 EJHL 5.

Fenton, Rachel Anne, Susan Heenan and Jane Rees, 'Finally Fit for Purpose? The Human Fertilization and Embryology Act 2008' [2010] 32(3) JSWFL 275.

Fenton, Rachel Anne, D Jane, V Rees and Sue Heenan, '"Shall I Be Mother?" Reproductive Autonomy, Feminism and the Human Fertilisation and Embryology Act 2008' in Jackie Jones, Anna, Michelle Fine and Adrienne Asch (eds), *Women with Disabilities: Essays in Psychology, Culture, and Politics* (Temple UP 1988).

Finck, Michèle and Betül Kas, 'Surrogacy Leave as a Matter of EU Law: *CD* and *Z*' [2015] 52(1) CML Rev 281.

Finger, Anne, *Past Due: A Story of Disability, Pregnancy and Birth* (Seal Press 1990).

Finkelstein, Vic, *A Personal Journey into Disability Politics* (Leeds University Centre for Disability Studies 2001) <https://disability-studies.leeds.ac.uk/wp-content/uploads/sites/40/library/finkelstein-presentn.pdf> accessed 18 July 2019.

Finkelstein, Vic, *The Social Model of Disability Repossessed* (Manchester Coalition of Disabled People 2001) <https://disability-studies.leeds.ac.uk/wp-content/uploads/sites/40/library/finkelstein-soc-mod-repossessed.pdf> accessed 18 July 2019.

Foubert, Petra, 'Child Care Leave 2.0 – Suggestions for the Improvement of the EU Maternity and Parental Leave Directives from a Rights Perspective' [2017] 24(2) MJ 245.

Fox, Carol, 'Protection in Contemplation of Pregnancy?' [2008] Emp LB 3.

Fox, Marie, 'The Human Fertilisation and Embryology Act 2008: Tinkering at the Margins' [2009] 17(3) Fem LS 333.

Francis, Leslie, Anita Silvers and Brittany Badesch, 'Women with Disabilities: Ethics of Access and Accommodation for Infertility Care' [2019] Ethical Issues in Women's Healthcare: Practice and Policy; University of Utah College of Law Research Paper <https://papers.ssrn.com/sol3/papers.cfm?abstract_id=3370556> accessed 18 July 2019.

Fredman, Sandra, 'A Difference with Distinction: Pregnancy and Parenthood Reassessed' [1994] 110(Jan) LQR 106.

Fredman, Sandra, 'Reversing Roles: Bringing Men into the Frame' [2014] 10(4) Int JLC 442.

Fredman, Sandra, 'Intersectional Discrimination in EU Gender Equality and Non-discrimination Law' (European Network of Legal Experts in Gender Equality and Non-discrimination, European Commission 2016).

Freeman, MDA, 'Towards a Critical Theory of Family Law' [1985] 38(1) CLP 153.

Grear, Rachel, Anne Fenton and Kim Stevenson (eds), *Gender, Sexualities and Law* (Routledge 2011).

Gilbert, Daphne and Diana Majury, 'Infertility and the Parameters of Discrimination Discourse' in Dianne Pothier and Richard Devlin (eds) *Critical Disability Theory: Essays in Philosophy, Politics, Policy and Law* (UBC Press 2006).

Greenberg, Judith G, 'The Pregnancy Discrimination Act: Legitimating Discrimination Against Pregnant Women in the Workforce' [1998] 50(2) Me L Rev 225.

Greil, Arthur, Julia McQuillan and Kathleen Slauson-Blevins, 'The Social Construction of Infertility' [2011] 5(8) Sociology Compass 736.

Hall, Kristina M, 'Pacourek v Inland Steel Company: Enforcing Equal Protection Rights by Designating Infertility as a Disability Under the American's with Disabilities Act' [1997] 11(2) BYU J Pub L 287.

Hannett, Sarah, 'Equality at the Intersections: The Legislative and Judicial Failure to Tackle Multiple Discrimination' [2003] 23(1) OJLS 65.

Healy, Connie, 'Once More with "Sympathy" but no Resolution for Intended Mothers: The EU, Ireland and the Surrogacy Dilemma' [2017] 39(4) JSWFL 504.

HM Treasury and Department for Business Innovation and Skills, 'The Plan for Growth' (March 2011).

Honeyball, Simon, 'Pregnancy and Sex Discrimination' [2000] 29(1) ILJ 43.

Horsey, Kirsty (ed), *Revisiting the Regulation of Human Fertilisation and Embryology* (Routledge 2015).

Horsey, Kirsty, 'Revisiting the Regulation of Human Fertilisation and Embryology' in Kirsty Horsey (ed), *Revisiting the Regulation of Human Fertilisation and Embryology* (Routledge 2015).

Hoskings, David L, 'A High Bar for Disability Rights' [2007] 36(2) ILJ 228.

Human Fertilisation and Embryology Authority, 'Fertility Treatment 2014–2016 Trends and Figures' (HFEA, March 2018).

Human Fertilisation and Embryology Authority, 'HEFA Fertility Treatment: Trends and Figures 2017' (HFEA 2019).

Iyer, Nitya, 'Categorical Denials: Equality Rights and the Shaping of Social Identity,' [1993] 19 Queen's LJ 179.

James, Grace, 'The Work and Families Act 2006: Legislation to Improve Choice and Flexibility?' [2006] 35(3) ILJ 272.

James, Grace, *The Legal Regulation of Pregnancy and Parenting* (Routledge-Cavendish 2009).

James, Grace, 'Mothers and Fathers as Parents and Workers; Family Friendly Employment Policies in an Era of Shifting Identities' [2009] 31(3) JSWFL 271.

Johnston, Timothy D, 'Reproduction Is Not a Major Life Activity: Implications for HIV Infection as a Per Se Disability under the Americans with Disabilities Act' [1999] 85 Cornell L Rev 189.

Kantola, Johanna and Kevät Nousiainen, 'Institutionalizing Intersectionality in Europe' [2009] 11(4) International Feminist Journal of Politics 459.

Kayess, Rosemary and Phillip French, 'Out of Darkness into Light? Introducing the Convention on the Rights of Persons with Disabilities' [2008] 8(1) HRL Rev 1.

Khetarpal, Abha and Satendra Singh, 'Infertility: Why Can't We Classify This Inability as Disability?' [2012] 5, 6 Australasian Medical Journal 334.

Kilpatrick, Claire, 'The ECJ and Labour Law: A 2008 Retrospective' [2009] 38(2) ILJ 180.

Krajewska, Atina, 'Access of Single Women to Fertility Treatment: A Case of Incidental Discrimination?' [2015] 23(4) Med L Rev 620.

Lanctot, Catherine J, 'Ad Hoc Decision Making and Per Se Prejudice: How Individualizing the Determination of Disability Undermines the ADA' [1997] 42(2) Vill L Rev 327.

Law Commission, *Thirteenth Programme of Law Reform* (Law Com No.377, 2017).

Lawson, Anna, 'Disability and Employment in the Equality Act 2010: Opportunities Seized, Lost and Generated' [2011] 40(4) ILJ 359.

Lourenço, Luísa and Pekka Pohjankoski, 'Breaking Down Barriers? The Judicial Interpretation of "Disability" and "Reasonable Accommodation" in EU Anti-Discrimination Law' in Uladzislau Belavusau and Kristin Henrard (eds), *EU Anti-Discrimination Law Beyond Gender* (Hart 2019).

Makkonen, Timo, 'Multiple, Compound and Intersectional Discrimination: Bringing the Experiences of the Most Marginalized to the Fore' (LLM thesis, Institute for Human Rights, Åbo Akademi University 2002).

McCandless, Julie and Sally Sheldon, 'The Human Fertilisation and Embryology Act (2008) and the Tenacity of the Sexual Family Form' [2010] 73(2) MLR 175.

McCarn, Alison A, 'Rights Not Charity: An Analysis of the Models of Disability and Their Contribution to the Construction and Interpretation of the Definition of Disability under the Disability Discrimination Act 1995' [2003] 6(2) CIL 103.

McColgan, Aileen, 'Reconfiguring Discrimination Law' [2007] (SPR) PL 74.

McCrudden, Christopher, *The New Concept of Equality* (ERA conference, Trier, 2–3 June 2003) <www.era-comm.eu/oldoku/Adiskri/02_Key_concepts/2003_McCrudden_EN.pdf> accessed 14 July 2019.

McGlynn, Clare, 'Ideologies of Motherhood in European Community Sex Equality Law' [2000] 6(1) ELJ 29.

Miller, Jeffery, 'The European Disability Rights Revolution' [2019] 44(1) EL Rev 67.

More, Gillian, 'Equal Treatment in European Community Law: The Limits of Market Equality' in Anne Bottomley (ed), *Feminist Perspectives on the Foundational Subjects of Law* (Cavendish Publishing Limited 1996).

Morris, Jenny, *Pride Against Prejudice* (The Women's Press 1991).

Morris, Jenny, 'Feminism and Disability' [1993] 43 Feminist Rev 57.

Mosoff, Judith, 'Reproductive Technology and Disability: Searching for the Rights and Wrongs in Explanation' [1993] 16 Dal LJ 98.

Neuvonen, Päivi Johanna, 'Inequality in Equality' in the European Union Equality Directives. A Friend or a Foe of More Systematized Relationships between the Protected Grounds?' [2015] 15(4) IJDL 222.

O'Donovan, Katherine, *Sexual Divisions in Law* (Weidenfeld and Nicolson 1985).

Office for Disability Matters, *Equality Act 2010 Guidance: Guidance on Matters to Be Taken into Account in Determining Questions Relating to the Definition of Disability* (HM Government 2011).

Oliver, Michael, 'A New Model of the Social Work Role in Relation to Disability' in Jo Campling (ed), *The Handicapped Person: A New Perspective for Social Workers* (Radar 1981).

Oliver, Michael, *Understanding Disability: From Theory to Practice* (2nd edn, Palgrave Macmillan 2009).

Oliver, Mike, 'Social Policy and Disability: Some Theoretical Issues' [1986] 1(1) Disability, Handicap & Society 5.

Oliver, Mike, 'The Social Model of Disability: Thirty Years On' [2013] 28(7) Disability & Society 1024.

Olsen, Frances E, 'The Family and the Market: A Study of Ideology and Legal Reform' [1983] 96(7) Harvard L Rev 1497.

Onufrio, Maria Vittoria, 'Intersectional Discrimination in the European Legal Systems. Toward a Common Solution?' [2014] 14(2) IJDL 126.

Payne, Nicola, Susan Seenan and Olga van den Akker, 'Experiences and Psychological Distress of Fertility Treatment and Employment' [2019] 40(2) Journal of Psychosomatic Obstetrics & Gynecology 156.

Powell, Lisa D, 'The Infertile Womb of God: Ableism in Feminist Doctrine of God' [2015] 65(1) Cross Currents 116.

Quinn, Gerard and Eilionóir Flynn, 'Transatlantic Borrowings: The Past and Future of EU Non-discrimination Law and Policy on the Ground of Disability' [2012] 60(1) Am J Comp L 23.

'Recent Cases Employment Law – Title VII – Seventh Circuit Allows Employee Terminated for Undergoing in Vitro Fertilization to Bring Sex Discrimination Claim. – Hall v. Nalco Co., 534 F.3d 644 (7th Cir. 2008) [2009] 122(5) Harvard L Rev 1533.

Rydel, Peter K, 'Redefining the Right to Reproduce: Asserting Infertility as a Disability under the Americans with Disabilities Act' [1999] 63 Alb L Rev 593.

Sainsbury, Diane, 'Women's and Men's Social Rights: Gendering Dimensions of Welfare States' in Diane Sainsbury (ed), *Gendering Welfare State Regimes* (Sage Publications 1994).

Sainsbury, Diane, *Gender, Equality and Welfare States* (CUP 1996).

Sato, Shorge, 'A Little Bit Disabled: Infertility and the Americans with Disabilities Act' [2001] 5 NYUJ Legis & Pub Pol'y 189.

Schiek, Dagmar, 'A New Framework on Equal Treatment of Persons in EC Law?' [2002] 8(2) Eur LJ 290.

Schiek, Dagmar, 'Broadening the Scope and the Norms of EU Gender Equality Law: Towards a Multidimensional Conception of Equality Law' [2005] 12(4) MJ 427.

Schiek, Dagmar, 'Executive Summary' in Susanne Burri and Dagmar Schiek (eds), *Multiple Discrimination in EU Law: Opportunities for Legal Responses to Intersectional Gender Discrimination?* (European Network of Legal Experts in the Field of Gender Equality 2007).

Schiek, Dagmar, 'Organizing EU Equality Law Around the Nodes of "Race", Gender and Disability' in Dagmar Schiek and Anna Lawson (eds), *European Union Non-Discrimination Law and Intersectionality: Investigating the Triangle of Racial, Gender and Disability Discrimination* (Ashgate Publishing 2011).

Schiek, Dagmar, 'Intersectionality and the Notion of Disability in EU Discrimination Law' [2016] 53 CML Rev 35.

Schiek, Dagmar, 'On Uses, Mis-uses and Non-uses of Intersectionality before the Court of Justice (EU)' [2018] 18(2–3) IJDL 82.

Schiek, Dagmar and Victoria Chege (eds), *European Union Non-discrimination Law, Comparative Perspectives on Multidimensional Equality Law* (Routledge-Cavendish 2009).

Schiek, Dagmar and Anna Lawson (eds), *European Union Non-Discrimination Law and Intersectionality: Investigating the Triangle of Racial, Gender and Disability Discrimination* (Ashgate Publishing 2011).

Schiek, Dagmar and Anna Lawson, 'Introduction' in Dagmar Schiek and Anna Lawson (eds), *European Union Non-Discrimination Law and Intersectionality: Investigating the Triangle of Racial, Gender and Disability Discrimination* (Ashgate Publishing 2011).

Schiek, Dagmar and Jule Mulder, 'Intersectionality in EU Law: A Critical Re-appraisal' in Dagmar Schiek and Anna Lawson (eds), *European Union Non-Discrimination Law and Intersectionality: Investigating the Triangle of Racial, Gender and Disability Discrimination* (Ashgate Publishing 2011)

Scotch, Richard K, 'Models of Disability and the Americans with Disabilities Act' [2000] 21 Berkeley J Emp & Lab L 213.

Scottish Law Commission, *Tenth Programme of Law Reform* (Law Com No.250, 2018).

Sen, Amartya, *Inequality Re-examined* (OUP 1992).

Shawrieh, Sherena, 'Bragdon v Abbott: Expanding the Reach of the Americans with Disabilities Act' [2000] 67(1) Defense Counsel Journal 106.

Sheldon, Alison, 'Women and Disability' in John Swain, Sally French, Colin Barnes and Carol Thomas (eds), *Disabling Barriers – Enabling Environments* (2nd edn, Sage 2004).

Shultz, Marjorie Maguire, 'Reproductive Technology and Intent-Based Parenthood: An Opportunity for Gender Neutrality' [1990] Wis L Rev 297.

Sternke Elizabeth A and Kathleen Abrahamson, 'Perceptions of Women with Infertility on Stigma and Disability' [2015] 33(3) Sex Disability 3.

Teresa, M, 'Working Women Seeking Infertility Treatments: Does the ADA or Title VII Offer Any Protection?' [2009] 58(1) Drake L Rev 295.

Thomas, Carol, 'The Baby and the Bath Water: Disabled Women and Mother-hood in Social Context' [1997] 19(5) Sociology of Health and Illness 622.

Thomas, Carol, 'How Is Disability Understood? An Examination of Sociological Approaches' [2004] 19(6) Disability & Society 569.

Tomei, Manuela, 'Discrimination and Equality at Work: A Review of the Concepts' [2003] 142(2) Int'l Lab Rev 397.

Tomkowicz, Sandra M, 'The Disabling Effects of Infertility: Fertile Grounds for Accommodating Infertile Couples under the Americans with Disabilities Act' [1995] 46 Syracuse L Rev 1051.

UN, Standard Rules on the Equalization of Opportunities for Persons with Disabilities, General Assembly Resolution 48/96 of 20 December 1993, UN Dec A/RES/48/96.

Van der Burch, Kerry, 'Courts' Struggle with Infertility: The Impact of *Hall v. Nalco* on Infertility-Related Employment Discrimination' [2010] 81 University of Colorado L Rev 545.

Vauchez, Stéphanie Hennette, 'The Society for the Protection of Unborn Children v. Grogan: Rereading the Case and Retelling the Story of Reproductive Rights in Europe' in Nicola Fernanda and Bill Davies (eds), *EU Law Stories: Contextual and Critical Histories of European Jurisprudence* (CUP 2017).

Verloo, Mieke, 'Multiple Inequalities, Intersectionality and the European Union' [2006] 13(3) EJWS 211.

Waddington, Lisa, 'Future Prospects for EU Equality Law: Lessons to Be Learnt from the Proposed Equal Treatment Directive' [2011] 36(2) EL Rev 163.

Waddington, Lisa, 'Saying All the Right Things and Still Getting It Wrong: The Court of Justice's Definition of Disability and Non-discrimination Law' [2015] 22(4) MJ 576.

Waddington, Lisa, 'The Influence of the UN Convention on the Rights of Persons with Disabilities on EU Anti-Discrimination Law' in Uladzislau Belavusau and Kristin Henrard (eds), *EU Anti-Discrimination Law Beyond Gender* (Hart 2019).

Weicker, Lowell P Jr, 'Historical Background of the Americans with Disabilities Act' [1991] 64 Temp L Rev 387.

Weldon-Johns, Michelle, 'From Modern Workplaces to Modern Families – Re-envisioning the Work – Family Conflict' [2015] 37(4) JSWFL 395.

Wenbourne, Nick, 'Disabled Meanings: A Comparison of the Definitions of Disability in the British Disability Discrimination Act of 1995 and the Americans with Disabilities Act of 1990' [1999] 23(1) Hastings Int'l & Comp L Rev 149.

Wilkinson, Wendy, 'Judicially Crafted Barriers to Bringing Suit under the Americans with Disabilities Act' [1997] 38 S Tex L Rev 907.

Wintemute, Robert, 'When Is Pregnancy Discrimination Indirect Sex Discrimination?' [1998] 27(1) ILJ 23.

Xenidis, Raphaële, 'Multiple Discrimination in EU Anti-Discrimination Law. Towards Redressing Complex Inequality?' in Uladzislau Belavusau and Kristin Henrard (eds), *EU Anti-Discrimination Law Beyond Gender* (Hart 2019).

Index

For Product Safety Concerns and Information please contact our EU
representative GPSR@taylorandfrancis.com
Taylor & Francis Verlag GmbH, Kaufingerstraße 24, 80331 München, Germany

www.ingramcontent.com/pod-product-compliance
Ingram Content Group UK Ltd.
Pitfield, Milton Keynes, MK11 3LW, UK
UKHW021423080625
459435UK00011B/134